D1434488

13153

1,000 Ideas by 100 Fashion Designers

ROCKPORT

1,000 Ideas by
100 Fashion Designers

Carolina Cerimedo

BEVERLY MASSACHUSETTS

ROCKPORT
PUBLISHERS

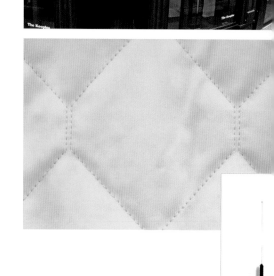

Copyright © 2010 by **maomao** publications
First published in 2010 in the United States of America by
Rockport Publishers, a member of
Quayside Publishing Group
100 Cummings Center
Suite 406-L
Beverly, MA 01915-6101
Telephone: (978) 282-9590
Fax: (978) 283-2742
www.rockpub.com

ISBN-13: 978-1-59253-572-9
ISBN-10: 1-59253-572-0

10 9 8 7 6 5 4 3 2 1

Publisher: Paco Asensio
Editorial coordination: Anja Llorella Oriol
Editor: Carolina Cerimedo
Text: Carolina Cerimedo (introduction), Cristian Campos, Macarena San Martín, Matteo Cossu
Art director: Emma Termes Parera
Layout: Esperanza Escudero
English translation: Cillero & de Motta

Editorial project:
maomao publications
Via Laietana, 32, 4th fl, of. 104
08003 Barcelona, Spain
Tel.: +34 93 268 80 88
Fax: +34 93 317 42 08
www.maomaopublications.com

Printed in China

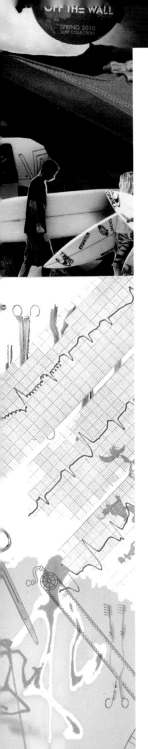

Contents

Generation F   8

1,000 Ideas   18

Adriana Degreas   20
Alejandra Quesada   23
Alena Akhmadullina   26
Alessia Giacobino/Jo No Fui   29
Alexandre, Laurent, Raphael Elicha/The Kooples   32
Alexi Freeman   35
Allegra Hicks   38
Aminaka Wilmont   41
Antonio Miró   44
Avsh Alom Gur   47
Bora Aksu   50
Bruce Montgomery   53
Bryce d'Anicé Aime   56
Carlota Santamaria, Susana Del Sol/just4fun   59
Carlotta Costanzo/Fiorucci   62
Carolin Lerch/Pelican Avenue   65
Carolina Ainstein/Lazaro, Jet   68
Céline Kamara-Gouge/Touch Luxe   71
Clea Garrick, Nathan Price/Limedrop   74
Cora Groppo   77
David Saunders/David David   80
Delphine Papiernik/Kickers   83
Elena Martín/Martin Lamothe   86
Estrella Archs   89
Eva Riu, Alberto Gabari/The Mystic Onion   92
Evangelina Bomparola   95
Eymèle Burgaud   98
Gaspard Yurkievich   101
Gemma Slack   104

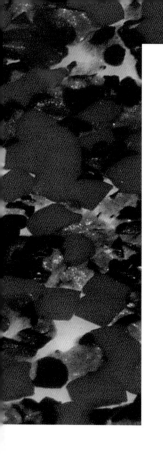

Georg Hieber — 107
Geraldine Cunto/La Martina — 110
Gori de Palma — 113
Gustavo Lins — 116
Harry Halim — 119
Igor Chapurin — 122
Imane Ayissi — 125
Inés Aguilar, Iván Martínez/La Casita de Wendy — 128
Iris van Herpen — 131
Isaac Fabregat, Manuel Olarte/Isaacymanu — 134
Isabela Capeto — 137
Ivana Helsinki — 140
Jane McMillan/Mac Millan — 143
Jasmin Shokrian — 146
Jessica Trosman — 149
Joanna Mastroianni — 152
Juan Vidal — 155
Juanita Álvarez — 158
Junko Shimada — 161
Karen Walker — 164
Kathleen König/Haltbar — 167
Krizia Robustella — 170
Lambert Perera Cortés, Sibylle Genin/Baron Baronne — 173
Laura Fontán, Diego Cortizas/chula — 176
Lidija Kolovrat — 179
Lívia Torres, Helena Pimenta/Amonstro — 182
Livia Ximénez-Carrillo, Christine Pluess/mongrels in common — 185
Llamazares y de Delgado — 188
Louise Amstrup — 191
Manuel Bolaño — 194
Marc Einsiedel, Julia Kleinwächter/Woolwill — 197
Mark Haskins/Vans — 200
Mark Liu — 203
Mattijs van Bergen — 206
MJ Diehl, Roman Milisic/House of Diehl — 209
Monique Collignon — 212
Mony Rivas/Chocolate — 215

Patricia Viera	218
Petar Petrov	221
Rafe Totengco/Rafe New York	224
Raphael Hauber/Postweiler Hauber	227
Rikkemai Nielsen/Stories	230
Rozalb de Mura	233
Sairah Hicks/Evie Belle	236
Samantha Pleet	239
Sandrina Fasoli, Michael Marson/Sandrina Fasoli	242
Sarah Swash, Toshio Yamanaka/Swash	245
Serge Cajfinger/Paule Ka	248
Shenan Anddrommeda Fraguadas	251
Sia Dimitriadi	254
Simone Nunes	257
Sonia Serlenga/adidas	260
Sophie Hulme	263
Spon Diogo	266
Steve J & Yoni P	269
Susanne Guldager	272
Takuya Miyama, Tomoko Kamijima/near.nippon	275
Thierry Lasry	278
Tom Scott	281
Tony Cohen	284
Tracey Mitchell, Leigh Mitchell/Dahlia	287
Txell Miras	290
Valentino	293
Victorio & Lucchino	296
Vidler & Nixon	299
Vincent Schoepfer	302
Virginia Spagnuolo/Divia Shoes	305
Willy Fantin, Andreas Doering/Heidi.com	308
Yiorgos Eleftheriades	311
Yiyí Gutz	314
Zazo & Brull	317

Who and what do you think about when you design?

Describe your mannequin and your workplace

When you **start** a collection, do you **think** about themes and **sensations**?

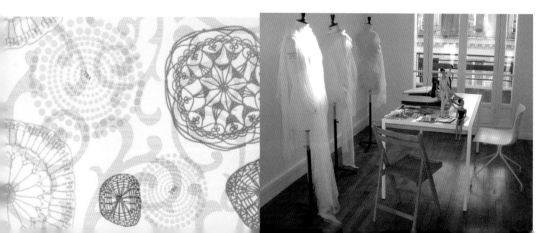

How do you translate the concept of the collection to each **item** you design?

Generation F

I've always seriously doubted that I chose the right career. Journalists have to limit themselves to the facts, while I work with my imagination, or at least ideas. My job is supposed to involve giving an account of the world around me with empirical precision—whereas I live in a parallel universe through the looking glass. As an editor, I always have to face my fears, and maybe (I did say

I have brought together 100 designers who have had an "intimate experience" with fashion and lived to tell the tale.

maybe) deal with my biggest one: making a decision. Because that's what editors do, they use their judgment and pick out which button should be used from a mass of others. They have access to the entire range and filter it down until they shortlist the options. They use a firm hand to spell out the message that the public will hear.

This time, I had to choose 100 fashion designers. It didn't matter whether they were new on the scene or signed autographs for their fans; whether they did business or art; whether they did haute couture or doodled on T-shirts; whether they began with a course project or ended up as a multinational; whether their labels had gray hairs or were pumping hormones; whether they showed in Paris or did the samba in Rio; whether they lived in Milan or a tiny Gaucho village in Argentina; whether they had a flagship store on Fifth Avenue or a showroom in a garage. I have brought together 100 designers who have had an "intimate experience" with fashion and lived to tell the tale. The aim of this book is to make the direct experience of these 100 designers a vicarious experience for new graduates: a system of learning whose main resource is the feelings and emotions of their fellow designers. It asks them questions like what they think about when they begin a collection; what kind of woman they have in mind when they design; what they have on their work table; how they transfer the concept for a season to each garment and accessory; why they choose a fabric and where they buy it; what they look for in color; whether they go for tradition or experimentation; what brand values they offer; how much importance they place on communication; what they change and leave unchanged in their style each year; whether they welcome or reject trends; what good habits they have; what bad habits they try to shake off; and whether their inspiration takes a back seat to sales. These are some of the many questions stu-

…a system of learning whose main resource is the feelings and emotions of their fellow designers.

dents ask themselves, and this book offers 1,000 answers. In order to succeed, there's no secret magic formula like Coca Cola's. But there is an almost unanimous feeling among designers: creative freedom while staying true to your own style can be the password that opens up Ali Baba's cave (or your bank account) for a sustainable and long-lasting label. In fashion, as in life, it seems that triumph comes to those who don't betray their ideals. After all, numbers aside, those who design fashion are seeking the same things as those who use it: self-expression.

Introspection

Before letting the fashion designers speak for themselves, this prologue takes in the ideas of the other professionals in the sector who are vital to a label's success or failure. Designers are not alone in the world like the Little Prince. They are not the only ones responsible for whether their label goes boom or bust. The ecosystem is completed with magazine editors, stylists, coolhunters, and buyers with the last word on the value of a collection. How does an outfit get to be on the cover of *Vogue*? How does *Glamour* decide on changes in its columns? How is it that one piece becomes the season's must-have?

"For a fashion designer to succeed, individuality is very important, but it should be linked to novelty. The key is to repeat the essence of a brand in another way each season; to reinterpret the label's trademarks. Vivienne Westwood is famous for

> "For a fashion designer to succeed, individuality is very important, but it should be linked to novelty."

high waists and asymmetrical dresses, but they are always different!" says Eva Sonaike, the fashion editor of *Elle* Germany. She also goes on to say, "I value being able to recognize all of those personal details in a designer and relating them with past work. We see them in Chanel and its tweed, which is repeated in every collection but in a different style—sometimes punk, other times retro. It's good to be surprised."

It's obvious that there can't be success when there is no one buying: "Designers should make their product desirable and comfortable. Clothes make the person and a good designer is capable of offering a collection that the public is reflected in. It's not a good thing to follow trends; the fashion factor will always be present. The most important thing is the clothes and to be able to provide your clients with what they are looking for, like a pair of high heels to make them feel sexy. So, depending on how buyers feel, they will choose between a Dior and a vintage piece." For the editor of this leading women's magazine, success is also connected to professional attitude. "Design must be seen as the responsibility of a job, but it should also be remembered that fashion isn't everything. It shouldn't be taken so seriously in a world where people are dying of hunger."

> The most important thing is the clothes and to be able to provide your clients with what they are looking for.

Why do you **choose** a certain fabric and where do you buy it? What type would you never use and why?

Do you **prefer** tradition or experimentation in **manufacturing**?

Who is your right arm?

What do you **look** to find in **color**?

Do you think it's **good** to develop a representative item in your **collection**?

VICTORIO & LUCCHINO

What are your **message** and communication **strategy**?

KicKers®

D LEFT, RIGHT

GORI DE PALMA
spring - summer 2009

Do you think your **creations** invoke **individuality** or group belonging?

What does your brand **name** promise?

Is **communication** important for **you**? Are you in charge of it **?**

The Koople

Leïla & Thomas en couple depuis

Be news

With regard to publishing criteria for labels to appear in her magazine, Eva is frank when she says that everything in the media revolves around advertising. "I'd like to have the freedom to promote to young designers, but I can't. If you want to see new talent, you should read independent magazines." This is the case of the New York publication *V* (short for *Visionaire Magazine*) that hit the newsstands in 1991 to feature the cutting edge in fashion and photography. For Diego Flores, publisher of the new edition of the legendary *V* in Spanish, the parameters of newsworthiness are found in the product itself. "For a designer to become part of a fashion or to feature in a magazine report, we look at the quality of the clothes, the creativity involved, and the innovation to be seen in the fabrics and cut."

"There are many factors to take into account when it comes to choosing an outfit for the cover. However, what we feature most in *Seventeen* are accessories. And for them to be on the assignment desk they have to be original and fun. They need to uphold the magazine's fresh image, and if they also set a trend, so much the better," explains Laura Vigo, publishing director for Argentina. In fact, innovation is a condition for a designer to appear in the media. "The media should consider their readers' interest with regard to what is a novelty. Our work is to know what our public's taste is so as to recognize when an up-and-coming talent has a chance of becoming a favorite. A young designer who knows how to interpret the desires of a generation or who knows how to trigger a new fashion is surely going to have good media exposure." A magazine focusing on teens is the most permeable space for independent designers, owing to the weakness young female readers feel for the latest. "Teenage girls are in the full process of putting a style together; they are looking for an identity and need variety. A single look in *Seventeen* can play a piece by a well-known designer against one by a newcomer. It's all about trying, but guided by the magazine, which represents an expert authorized to show new talent."

Rosane Ribeiro, journalist for *Vogue* Brazil and who trained as a fashion consultant, prefers to stand aside from the currents everyone follows and asserts the fact that she has the freedom to do it. "When I write a report, my choice of designers is based on their originality. When I say original, I don't mean something bizarre that no one is going to wear; I mean something different and beautiful at the same time, something that the English know how to do very well." Rosane shows her business side with this statement: "Don't forget that this product might be found in every brand of clothing, but in certain ones it is desirable, and people want to have it and want to use it. This is the impression I get from Burberry."

> "For a designer to become part of a fashion or to feature in a magazine report, we look at the quality of the clothes, the creativity involved, and the innovation to be seen in the fabrics and cut."

> "A young designer who knows how to interpret the desires of a generation or who knows how to trigger a new fashion is surely going to have good media exposure."

The ends that justify the means

At the same time, clothes enable people to assert their individuality and join the group they want to belong to. Fashion works two ways–for personal differentiation and for group acceptance. "People try to identify with a lifestyle through fashion; it's a cultural code. You only have to look at how someone dresses to know what group they belong to. All of this social meaning depends on where you come from and where you live. For example, in Brazil fashion is used to show the purchasing power you have," Rosane concludes. English buyer Abi Fisher has another perspective. She points out to consumer behavior based on the use of clothes rather than their meaning. "I look more at what my client needs instead of what the market decides. My public lives in the country, surrounded by cows and sheep, and therefore their way of dressing isn't governed by fashion but by

Abi Fisher points out consumer behavior based on the use of clothes rather than their meaning: "I look more at what my client needs instead of what the market decides."

comfort and quality. This is also my rule book for choosing the collections I buy and that's why I'm interested in labels like Max Mara and Temperley London."

What stylist Nao Koyabu chooses for her columns in the Japanese magazines *Fudge* and *So-En* is what she would wear herself. "I look for beauty. The Japanese are great followers of fashion icons. They want you to show them and suggest a way of styling to them. They look to Paris first, then New York." Contrary to the widespread belief that stylists show favoritism, it should be said that genuine publications try to transmit style; even when they are corrupt, they work like a catalog of the brands that are close to the magazine. Laura Saint Agne describes her styling work: "Whenever I have a production ahead of me, I think of what concept I'm going to use, what story I want to tell, and from those thread links I choose the labels. I select the designers whose clothes go with what I want to say." With the results of her photo sessions published in magazines such as *Fashion TV, Brando,* and *Playboy,* she explains that for a label to be featured in her columns, they must also have an identity and a level of experimentation, two values to highlight and communicate.

"Whenever I have a production ahead of me, I think of what concept I'm going to use, what story I want to tell, and from those thread links I choose the labels. I select the designers whose clothes go with what I want to say."

Do you feel **the need to improve yourself** every six months?

What does your **style** retain and what does it lose **from** time to time?

Does fashion come from the street or from a designer proposal?

Do you **make** art ?

What makes for **good sales?** Does this **influence** your creativity **?**

What is the best **praise** for **your** work?

What good **habits** should a designer **have?**

What is the best **lesson** you've received and that you'd like **to pass on?**

The future cannot repeat the past

"I give the same importance to new labels as I do to well-established ones. I don't discriminate. If their concept goes with the language I use or the message I want to convey, I don't take careers into account. Laura concludes by saying, "When I work with the media, I have the means of giving a boost to whoever needs it most. And in this way, I can collaborate with new generations of professionals who want to gain a foothold in this world that always feeds on new trends."

In this golden age for emergent talents, I enter the New Gen shows at London Fashion

> "When I work with the media, I have the means of giving a boost to whoever needs it most. And in this way, I can collaborate with new generations of professionals."

Week, and I can confirm the opportunity for independent designers in this space sponsored by Topshop. The sign on the wall explains the cause: This is an initiative to showcase the work of new artists, to collaborate in the production of their collections, and to give them international status. London has a reputation for being the capital of the most innovative fashion, and for the British Fashion Council this title of honor is mainly the fruit of its emerging talent and for its famous fashion schools. The phenomenon of seeking out novelty has multiplied in these times of recession, when the media and buyers are looking for something different to show in order to encourage cautious consumers to buy, given that now they won't spend without good reason.

For Kevin Tallon, editor of the book *Trends from Central Saint Martins* and a member of the institution's design laboratory, "A good fashion designer should have the intrinsic skill of showing the right designs at the right time; as well as the ability to foresee the near future, or at least to feel it. This key virtue, which unfortunately can't be taught, is essential for a designer to be trendy." But, what exactly is a trend? It's a hypothesis about future consumer behavior latent in different spheres of reality. Knowing this specific look to be followed by the masses puts the designer in the right place and time when it comes to designing. Although designing when thinking of trends doesn't guarantee sales, it at least enables production to take demand into account. So then, what comes first–the chicken or the egg, the designer or the street? "Creativity usually arises from a dialogue between designers, fashion leaders, and the consumers of fashion. The most influential labels create a wide range of looks. Among those are some that will become the must-haves of the season. This will happen because the press, style gurus, and trendsetters will pick them up and recommend them until they become the look of the season."

What is said about our coming into the world alone may be true, but what they say about our being alone in it is *not*. Everything is interconnected in a giant Lego set that

> "Creativity usually arises from a dialogue between designers, fashion leaders, and the consumers of fashion."

our visual culture makes a game of. If "sex, drugs, and rock & roll" were three words from a decade, "fashion" is the word for this time when designers are reproduced without the need for artificial insemination. Coco Chanel would lie on the floor to check a hem. On the contrary (and free of vertigo), I go on the London Eye...perhaps an aerial view of this "hyper-designed" society will help me to choose the designers for the next book.

1,000 Ideas

001 REFERENCES. When I'm designing, I dive into the universe of a very glamorous and strong woman: she is desired, she "pays her own bills," and she is full of attitude and faults as well. Then I trace a profile of this imaginary woman–how she would be, where she would go, her attitude, and her lifestyle. I also search inspiration in the women of the seventies, especially in Slim Aarons photography.

002 DEVELOPING A COLLECTION. I translate it to exalting the female figure and her curves in a sexy but subtle way, using pattern resources. The waist and the bum are always highlighted, the breasts are very structured.

003 COLORS. I'm always using cold, cool colors, and I look for elegance in them. The brand DNA is on the colors, on the design, on the avant-garde.

004 YOUR RIGHT ARM? My patternmakers.

005 INDIVIDUALITY VS. GROUP BELONGING. Definitely individuality, because my creations are authoritative and very exclusive. They're not for all women.

006 STYLE. Always be on the front of any proposal I suggested before overcoming myself.

007 IS FASHION ART? No, actually I don't understand it very much.

008 STREET FASHION VS. FASHION DESIGNER. Fashion for me comes from the world, comes from a situation, from an emotion, from a desire.

009 GOOD HABITS. A designer has to always overcome himself, and sometimes "bad habits" are a part of the creative process.

010
ADVICE. The lesson I've learned is to be determined and to believe in your history always. It's also very important when you're a designer to work every day on the whole process, from the fabric selection up to the final product. Otherwise, it gets more complicated and you lose heart.

001

Adriana Degreas
www.adrianadegreas.com.br

After a degree at FAAP (Armando Alvares Penteado Foundation), Brazilian designer Adriana Degreas started her career in fashion. She was immersed in this world since childhood: her grandfather dealt textiles and her grandmother owned a great number of garments by the most famous designers. Following her husband, who was the head of a beach fashion company on the market for more than 60 years, her passion started to take form. From this experience she learned more advanced production techniques. In 2001 came the decision to glamorize bikinis and start her own authorial project under her own name. Her inspiration is and has always been the intense feeling of what it means to be a woman. She spasmodically strives for perfection in all of her creations.

002

Alejandra Quesada
www.alejandraquesada.com

Alejandra Quesada was born in Mexico 27 years ago. She studied design at institutions of the likes of ESMOD University, Paris; IESModa, Mexico City; and Central Saint Martins College, London. After working for designers Isabel Marant in Paris, and Taka-Naka and Alexander McQueen in London, Alejandra Quesada presented her own collections at the London, Paris, and Mexico City Fashion Weeks. Alejandra Quesada defines her style as "happy colors for happy people," and likes to involve herself directly in the garments she designs.

She finds inspiration in nature–plants, flowers, birds, fruit, and other elements, which she tends to interpret as the obvious influence of Mexican textiles. Her designs feature hand embroidery, ornamentation, and a great attention to detail.

011 INSPIRATION. When I start a collection, I think of both themes and feelings; I don't limit myself to one thing. I always start with the colors, textures, and materials of things that appear to me from day to day: a wall of a building, Mexican markets, books, stories, concerts, a landscape...

012 WORKPLACE. My table is a little messy; I have a lot of things. I do try to clean it, though. When I sketch, for some strange reason I end up on the floor. The floor is my giant table. A mannequin is one of the best tools for putting an idea down. My mannequin is the same one I started my career with ten years ago.

013 MATERIALS. Fabric is the base I start with. It's very difficult to find fabrics in Mexico. My solution is to buy very simple, basic, and plain cloth, making sure that it's of good quality. I then transform it. We dye the fabrics different colors; we print them, either by silk-screening them or digitally. We embroider them and we add appliqué. In other words, we customize them. It's fun to design the textiles so that you can create a silhouette with them later.

014 COLORS. I don't look for anything special in each, I just like to see how they look together. Mexico is a country filled with color and I always discover new combinations, whether on ice cream or a wall in Oaxaca, on traditional native clothing or on piñatas. Color is the reflection of light.

015 TRADITIONAL MANUFACTURING VS. EXPERIMENTATION. I like to experiment with traditional techniques, that is, to return to classical textile techniques. I then turn them around to create something new, with other volumes, materials, and applications.

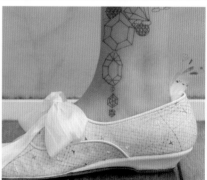

016 BRAND VALUES. More than make clothes, what Alejandra Quesada wants is to tell stories. She likes colors, music, flavors, textures, history, magic, and the universe.

017 IS FASHION ART? I don't know if what I'm doing is art, but what I am sure of is that it is a part of it. Painting, illustration, music, photography, cinema, theater, and dance are all collaborators. Fashion is connected to art and, like art, fashion is a way of speaking and expressing one's self.

018 GOOD HABITS. The habits a designer should have are order, perseverance, patience, and, above all, faith.

019 ACKNOWLEDGEMENT. I'm very shy and I don't like to come out at the end of a runway show. At my last showing, I decided to count to ten before appearing, and I realized in the end that the applause I received was what keeps me going.

020 COMMUNICATION. My strategy is to travel. Until today, the thing that has helped me most to grow has been to get out: taking part in showrooms in Paris and London, and having good PR in Japan.

021 MUSES. While I create lady's wear, I think about strong and independent women. My ideal is a woman out of age and out of time who decides the destiny of an epoch. Tilde Swinton, Björk, and Róisín Murphy are very close to me, all of them are modern icons of style and make an enormous impact on a fashion.

022 INSPIRATION. Each of my collections originates in a theme of Russian culture. First of all, I define the central axis of ideas: a historical era, a legend, or a work of art. After that, I adapt the chosen subjects under modern lines and directions.

023 MANNEQUIN. I prefer people from real life. It is much more interesting to observe and study their tastes and requirements. My girlfriends and my family are outstanding people who inspire me and are a source of my ideas.

024 DEVELOPING A COLLECTION. In each detail of my collection a certain ideology appears. The skill of the designer consists of making an unostentatious adaptation of the general theme to each separate unit. With this defined direction, you distribute forces so that each item supplements the other.

025 COLORS. It is one of the main points of a collection. The human eye, first of all, catches color, and only then it perceives forms, volumes, and details. For choosing the colors, follow your own sensations. Feel the color, understand it, and afterwards create clothes. Search for a certain color palette and its combinations: experimentation is a must to achieve good results in this business.

026 BRAND VALUES. In general, the success of a brand directly depends on distribution. Therefore, on our more important projects, we hope to attract a greater number of clients through an expansion of stores and distribution. The opening of the first monobrand boutique of Alena Akhmadullina has recently taken place. I hope that in the near future we will take hold of the whole world.

027 YOUR RIGHT ARM? For a designer, team work is a very important point. I think that each designer should have a trusty, harmonious collective to count on. The generated command of adherents will only add to your success.

028 IS FASHION ART? Any fashion show is a certificate of modern art and self-expression. For the designer, the show must be a demonstration of uniqueness and it is an excellent chance to prove your identity. But there is also another collection, the one that the designer creates for sale, in which you should consult with buyers and experts in marketing.

029 ADVICE. Do not listen to requirements. Express yourself and show your unique world. The fashion industry functions in just the opposite: the offer gives rise to the demand. The designer should be sincere and always introduce something new. Only in this way can you be recognized.

030 STYLE. Each designer should have unique handwriting–that certain style that defines the concept of a brand. Mine is Russian subjects and I work with this direction in mind, diluting it with more universal tendencies. It is important to realize that uniformity and uniformity of a collection are absolutely different concepts. The designer should retain his style and at the same time not repeat it. Always be fresh.

003

Alena Akhmadullina
www.alenaakhmadullina.com

From 1995 to 2000 this young Russian designer studied at St. Petersburg State University of Technology and Design. From the very first year of her studies she created two collections annually. As a rule they were avant-garde collections. Her brand went on to become a unique example in the history of Russian and world design. She has become one of the main Russian newsmakers for glossies and fashion columnists in Moscow-Paris-Milan and other European fashion capitals. Akhmadullina showed her first seasonal prêt-à-porter collection during the Paris Fashion Week in fall 2005. Since that time she has demonstrated a new collection on the Paris runway every season, breaking stereotypes and changing the attitude toward Russia as a "far from fashion" country.

004

Alessia Giacobino/Jo No Fui
www.jonofui.it

Alessia Giacobino took the world by surprise in 2001 when she launched her label Jo No Fui and left opinion makers impressed with her sophistication and determination. The charm of this new label was, and continues to be, its individuality and distinction, and the overwhelming but vague way that it was radically chic. Giacobino designs feminine, elegant, and cutting-edge clothes, and they are set apart by their tailored fit, and the fact that they are only made using quality Italian fabrics. The exclusive nature of the collections is guaranteed by their impeccable made-in-Italy production and their limited and highly selective distribution. It is only possible to find them in particular stores, in the company of the world's leading luxury brands.

031 INSPIRATION. There is never a fixed starting point in my creativity: it can be a special item, a picture, a style icon. The first hint creates a theme that develops into a collection. The process is always nourished by every piece of input, from team work and brainstorming.

032 DEVELOPING A COLLECTION. The creative process is always linked with a deep styling contribution. My designs are meant for the style-conscious woman, with a strong character that likes to freely mix things up. The Jo No Fui collection is made up of different items that are easy to mix up. I do not want a Jo No Fui item to be recognized immediately and be stereotyped. I like my clothes to be defined as simply beautiful.

033 MATERIALS. Jo No Fui is an Italian brand and my main concern is to produce everything in Italy, all the way down to the fabrics. I'm lucky enough to have the best Italian fabric producers and this keeps the quality level high.

034 TRADITIONAL MANUFACTURING VS. EXPERIMENTATION. As a woman designer and after studying architecture I feel quite traditional. I also like to play with materials but I never go too extreme. I always work on representative items: the flare pant, the short tunic dress, the sporty boot, the wide embroidered shirt are my all-time favorites and I keep on proposing them in different fabrics and colors as my customers keep asking.

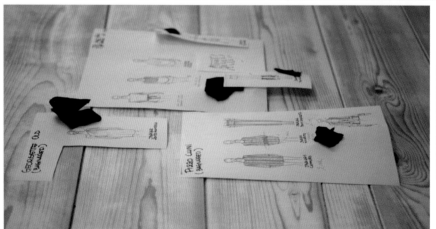

035 COMMUNICATION STRATEGY. My strategy is always to be in the best shops and this is proving to be a rewarding one.

036 BRAND VALUES. My collection represents myself as a woman and as a creative designer. My taste is represented in the collection. During the years this has raised interest and clients now choose Jo No Fui because they feel represented by the brand style. That is, starts as individuality and melts into a group of women with common interests and taste.

037 STYLE. One's style has a trace that shows in every collection, I do not like to throw anything away. I like the past and history's coming and going to be reflected in the collections I create.

038 IS FASHION ART? Sure, fashion is crafts. I chose a water mill as the workplace of the Jo No Fui team. Lost in the countryside near Rimini, the ancient mill facilities are still there and we just restored them with metalworks by Mutoid–a punk artists' community based in Rimini.

039 ADVICE. My grandfather told me once to always do your own things. He told me that the best way to learn your own lesson is to take your own risks, to always look ahead and to not care about critics. All power is in your will.

040 SALES. A good collection makes for good sales. I never follow pure creativity but I listen to my commercial instinct; so far that is paying back. I do long dresses if the collection goes on the catwalk with short, cropped skirts. I always create special items in the collection without pushing too far on creativity and price.

041 INSPIRATION. When we start a collection we generally put together some inspiration boards and images we really like that are taken from art, film, photography, and just real people in the street. At the end of the day we always aim to design stuff we want to wear ourselves.

042 DEVELOPING A COLLECTION. It's important to always be coherent to the universe we create. In all of our collections we always have the same codes and details—the overall feeling we want our brand to echo. Our signature identity can be seen through the following details: skullhead patches, skullhead blason buttons, handkerchief in the jacket breast pocket, and/or T-shirts, sometimes with black-and-white graphic prints on them.

043 COLORS. Color is very important to us. In each collection we try to maintain a certain subtle coherence in color. We generally like to pick one or two colors that really stand out, otherwise we want to maintain subtle grays, navy and, of course, black.

044 YOUR RIGHT ARM? My brothers are a huge influence. We all bring something different to the table. We create the brand together and enjoy doing it. It is the most important thing to enjoy creating; even if we all have different roles in the company, we make all decisions together.

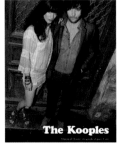

045
COMMUNICATION STRATEGY. For our advertising, we use real-life couples because who can represent your brand better than real people? Everyone can recognize themselves in our advertising. We are surrounded by top models that don't really look like real people and I think the customers are fed up with this kind of communication. It's the trademark of The Kooples: real life and real people.

The Kooples

Inna & Bak en couple depuis 4 mois

The Kooples

Lella & Thomas en couple depuis 2 ans

046 INDIVIDUALITY VS. GROUP BELONGING. We always like to promote individuality. Our collections are designed to permit people to mix and match according to their personalities. Because we always support individuality, we choose real couples and different personalities for our campaigns.

047 EVOLUTION. Fashion is a challenge, the competition is hard, so you always have to do better than the last collection. You always have to surprise the customer.

048 IS FASHION ART? For us, fashion comes from the street from real life, that's why we use real couples in our advertising campaigns. In the street, you see all kinds of things and overall you really see what people want. We are also very inspired by music, art, and vintage.

049 ADVICE. Work hard and enjoy yourself and the best will come out of you. Constantly ask yourself questions.

050 SALES. What makes for good sales is honesty, enjoying what we do, designing things we want to wear, and keeping our eyes open to suggestions, people, and life.

005

Alexandre, Laurent, Raphael Elicha/The Kooples
www.thekooples.com

This French label wants to be a breath of real life in the fashion world. This means reflecting the present state of mind felt in Paris and London, a trend in music, fashion as a statement, and a garment designed for two people, regardless of whether they have been together for five minutes, fifteen years, just for one night, or whether it is no more than a game–like life itself. The Kooples clothes are made from quality fabrics, with body hugging shapes, and are easily identified by their little details such as patches, skull buttons, handkerchiefs in jacket or shirt pockets, and black-and-white prints on T-shirts. They are perfect for dressing guys and girls from head to toe–for as long as they want to hang around.

© www.ashotaway.com

006

Alexi Freeman
www.alexifreeman.com

Based in Melbourne, Alexi is a fashion designer whose collections for women are manufactured locally, incorporating elements of hand-drawn and printed textiles worked into drape that is juxtaposed with tailoring. Freeman's eponymous label explores urbane elegance for modern women who are enamored by the past, but lust after the future. Having studied fine arts at the University of Tasmania, where he majored in printmaking and sculpture, Freeman's unorthodox approach provides his label with a strong point of difference that is earning him the attention of fashion industry and fashion public alike. Freeman's work is held in numerous private collections in Australia, Europe, and the US, and his work has been exhibited at shows in contemporary spaces such as Australian Galleries, Design Centre Center Launceston, and Queen Victoria Museum, among others.

051 INSPIRATION. I draw in an automatic way, intuitively sketching a free flow of new ideas. I then develop textile motifs and search for suitable fabrics to bring these initial ideas to life. I also think about the woman who will wear the collection, with the aim of offering a collection that is fresh, modern, wearable, and suitable for the climate of the market I am designing for.

052 WORKPLACE. I work in a small studio in Collingwood, Melbourne, Australia. Here I design and make samples, and although I check my toiles with a stand initially, I prefer to test the fit of my pieces on living, breathing women, not industry waifs mind you, but real women with real body shapes who are indicative of the clients who will eventually wear my clothes.

053 COLORS. I love working with gradations of colors throughout a collection and although most of our styles are ordered in shades of black, I really enjoy working with a tonal palette of highlight colors that accent and juxtapose the more commercial, darker shades.

054 DEVELOPING A COLLECTION. Once I have the design, the pattern made, and cut a new sample, I work closely with a print house, dye house, and sample machinist who interpret my print, color, and garment concepts and help realize my creative vision. Once the sample collection is complete, I then work with a sales agent to sell the collection. Finally I work with a manufacturing house to reproduce my designs for my clients.

055 STYLE. The Alexi Freeman brand promises: Deceptively simple, athletic functionality. Old school glamour with new school sass. Gallant femininity. Empyrean utilitarianism. Devil-may-care casual opulence and allure. To raise more than one pair of eyebrows. Ethically-made pieces that will stand the test of time. Directional collections that are not dictated by trends. And a lot of bang for your buck!

© www.ashotaway.com

© www.marniehaddad.com

056 COMMUNICATION STRATEGY. I am the designer of a small independent fashion label. Informed by my artisanal training, I design seasonal fashion collections of women's wear that are locally made and ethically produced. I work closely with an advertising agency that helps prepare our marketing collateral, and a press agent who assists us in communicating this material to media, wholesale buyers, and private clients.

057 EVOLUTION. Everyday is an opportunity for self-improvement. In terms of my collections, I analyze what has worked well for me in previous collections, whilst ceaselessly striving to forge new ground with the next. My philosophy is that fashion is a reflection of life, and life is always changing, so fashion must grow and change along with it to remain relevant.

058 IS FASHION ART? Formally trained in fine arts, I apply the skills I learned as an artist to the work I conceive as a fashion designer. Since making the switch from fine artist to fashion designer, people often ask if I will ever make art again, but for me there is little separation between the two. It's simply a case of realizing my creative energies in the wearable vernacular of fashion, rather than in the pursuit of art per se. I feel the artisanal basis of fashion is too often overlooked, but without its genesis in arts and crafts, fashion would not be the global phenomenon it is today.

059 ACKNOWLEDGEMENT. The best one is when clients tell me they had been looking everywhere for something, but could not find it until they came to my showroom—that is always a thrill: to know that there is a niche for what I do and that my work is relevant to the needs of the market. Also, I think being paid on time is a rather nice form of praise! But I always take my praise with a grain of salt.

060
ADVICE. A passion for fashion is not enough to survive in this industry. Granted it's a start, but you also need sharp business acumen, excellent time-management skills, a head full of ideas, and a never-say-die attitude. Not to mention a full bill of health!

© fashionising.com

061 REFERENCES. Women in history and women on the street.

062 WORKPLACE. Creative, homely, bright.

063 MATERIALS. I design my own fabrics and tend to use silks, cottons, velvets, wools–natural fibers.

064 YOUR RIGHT ARM? My team.

065 INDIVIDUALITY VS. GROUP BELONGING. Individuality.

066 STYLE. A strong determined woman who is at ease with her fragility and has a lot of style.

067 EVOLUTION. My work retains creative vocab; but sometimes loses outside perspective.

068 ADVICE. Discipline and perseverance.

069 ACKNOWLEDGEMENT. When a client is praised for looking good in one of my dresses!

070
GOOD HABITS. Never stop learning.

007

Allegra Hicks
www.allegrahicks.com

Allegra Hicks is the designer behind the eponymous luxury lifestyle brand that is now recognized around the world for its beautiful textiles and prints. Allegra grew up in Turin, Italy and studied design in Milan and fine arts in Brussels before moving to New York, where she started her career working in the arts. After having established her name in the world of interiors, Allegra moved into fashion design. Today Allegra Hicks designs two women's ready-to-wear and a cruise collection per year as well as a home collection, featuring houseware and linens, as well as an interior collection of fabrics, rugs, and wall papers. Allegra uses a unique print vocabulary and applies this to all her collections: fashion, home, and interior. Her style can be described as timelessly elegant, sophisticated, organic, and eclectic, often with a vintage feel.

008

Aminaka Wilmont
www.aminakawilmont.com

Inspired by the conceptual work of photographers Idris Khan, Pau Ardid, and Tim Walker, Aminaka Wilmont's F/W 09 collection is themed by the notion of time. Its style continually evokes a sense of intimacy, memories, and emotion in the observer. Luxurious fabrics are used to reflect the concepts that inspire the clothes. Visually challenging, colorful graphics and digitally enhanced prints capture the transient theme of its garments beautifully. They are fond of details, including laser-etched vertebrae and intricate Excella zip accessories, which perfectly fuse innovation and design. With industry affirmation (Fashion Fringe), and continued success with Net-a-Porter, Aminaka Wilmont is firmly established as one of the fashion world's most interesting and creative brands.

071 INSPIRATION. All of our collections evolve around a theme that guides every aspect within the collection.

072 MUSES. It differs from season to season and depends on our mood and direction–ultimately we think about "our" woman in the form of a muse.

073 WORKPLACE. Our studio is small and usually looks like a creative maelstrom of samples and designs scattered all over. We have 12 white mannequins in the studio that are in constant use.

074 MATERIALS. We evaluate what we need the fabric to do for the design to work in the best possible way and make the selection thereafter. We source from everywhere around the globe but usually end up using materials from UK or Asia.

075 TRADITIONAL MANUFACTURING VS. EXPERIMENTATION. Experimentation– without a doubt! To have a representative item that people can associate the collection with and remember it by is a useful tool.

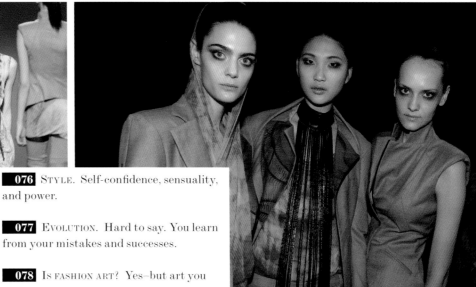

076 STYLE. Self-confidence, sensuality, and power.

077 EVOLUTION. Hard to say. You learn from your mistakes and successes.

078 IS FASHION ART? Yes–but art you can wear.

079 STREET FASHION VS. FASHION DESIGNER. I am not sure I understand the difference. Designers pick up their inspiration from the streets and the general feel of the time.

080 COMMUNICATION STRATEGY. Be unashamed of who you are.

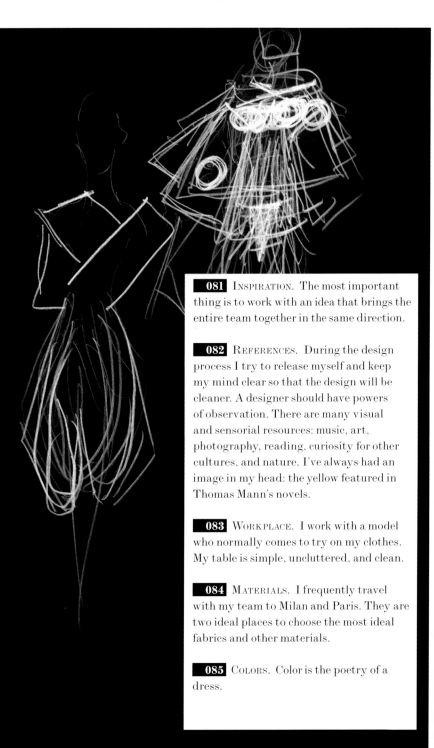

081 INSPIRATION. The most important thing is to work with an idea that brings the entire team together in the same direction.

082 REFERENCES. During the design process I try to release myself and keep my mind clear so that the design will be cleaner. A designer should have powers of observation. There are many visual and sensorial resources: music, art, photography, reading, curiosity for other cultures, and nature. I've always had an image in my head: the yellow featured in Thomas Mann's novels.

083 WORKPLACE. I work with a model who normally comes to try on my clothes. My table is simple, uncluttered, and clean.

084 MATERIALS. I frequently travel with my team to Milan and Paris. They are two ideal places to choose the most ideal fabrics and other materials.

085 COLORS. Color is the poetry of a dress.

086
MANUFACTURING VS
ESPERIMENTATION.
Experimentation requires
tradition. The signature piece isn't
looked for, it normally appears.

087 YOUR RIGHT ARM? My right hand is, of course, Gabriel González. He's always been with me. He's my support and the person I trust with all parts of the business.

088 BRAND VALUES. My label promises nothing. But I'm satisfied if wearing my clothes makes people feel good.

089 PHILOSOPHY. By definition, fashion is democratic because it spreads.

090 ADVICE. My father told me one day, "half of life is dirtiness and the other half is cleanliness." Remembering this has balanced me. You should never stop working out of love and humility, and keep in mind that it's a luxury to see people comfortably wearing the clothes that you have thought up.

009

Antonio Miró
www.antoniomiro.es

Since 1986 when Ignacio Malet, Fernando Zallo, and Antonio Miró started out, their company has had nothing but success: it was awarded the Cristóbal Balenciaga Prize for Best Spanish Designer in 1987; it designed the wardrobe for Barcelona Olympic Games staff members in 1992; it designed the new curtain for the stage at the Liceu opera house in 1997, it received the FAD Medal for career in 2000; and won the 2001 prize for best F/W collection at the Pasarela Cibeles runway shows in Madrid in 2001. Antonio Miró collections have also appeared at numerous fashion runway events in Paris, Milan, Florence, Tokyo, and New York. Antonio Miró currently designs men's and women's collections, sold and distributed directly to his own stores in Spain (Barcelona, Madrid, and Bilbao) and in Japan.

010 Avsh Alom Gur
www.avshalomgur.com

London-based designer Avsh Alom Gur studied in Central Saint Martins, graduating in 2002 with a distinction in the MA fashion course. From then on, Gur worked with various leading fashion houses, consulting for brands like Chloé, Donna Karan, Roberto Cavalli, and Nicole Farhi while honing his skills and gaining great insight and experience into the fashion industry to finally launch his own label in 2005. Receiving the Top Shop New Gen Award on the same year for sponsored stands, Gur made his debut in London Fashion Week at the Natural History Museum. This time however, Gur also made his debut off-schedule catwalk show at On|Off at the Royal Academy of Arts receiving an overwhelming reception for his collection of wrap tops, evening and baby-doll dresses, and ponchos that incorporate hand-carved, semi-precious stones inspired by the Bedouin tribes.

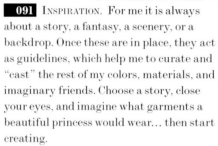

091 INSPIRATION. For me it is always about a story, a fantasy, a scenery, or a backdrop. Once these are in place, they act as guidelines, which help me to curate and "cast" the rest of my colors, materials, and imaginary friends. Choose a story, close your eyes, and imagine what garments a beautiful princess would wear… then start creating.

092 WORKPLACE. It is an organized chaos. Masses of fabrics, materials, and equipment hanging from the ceiling alongside objects found in the streets. It is an open space which hosts both creative and technical staff.

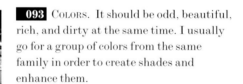

093 COLORS. It should be odd, beautiful, rich, and dirty at the same time. I usually go for a group of colors from the same family in order to create shades and enhance them.

094 BRAND VALUES. My label evokes innovation, creativity, perfected imperfection, and fun.

095
MATERIALS. I love fabrics that are made from natural fibers such as cotton, linen, and silk. I usually buy fabrics in markets at relatively affordable prices. I then manipulate them with silkscreen printing, over-dyeing, and distressing, according to my needs. Any preprinted fabrics which carry other designer imagery would never be found in my studio.

096 COMMUNICATION STRATEGY. Make something beautiful and do it with love, care, and attention. Give it some time and then people will respond to it.

097 EVOLUTION. For me, fashion is about evolution and not revolution. Every collection is a new challenge in which I aspire to reach new heights.

098 PHILOSOPHY. Art is in the eye of the beholder. I create fashion, I create clothes, I create products that can be worn. In extreme occasions some items can be admired and therefore can be classified as art.

099 ADVICE. Do not take any stress, do not give any stress. Think inside the box.

100 ACKNOWLEDGEMENT. The best praise for me is to have my art featured in printed publications, because these pages will stay long after I have gone.

101
WORKPLACE. My workplace is my hidden cocoon and it's very personal. My workshop is like the kitchen of a restaurant. It's the actual reality and it's where all the ideas take place. The workshop needs to have the characteristics of its designer.

102 INSPIRATION. Where you live and what you see daily is necessary for inspirational reference. I try to use it as a tool instead of a crutch. I usually start with a thought, an idea, a concept, or a image. Other times, I will begin with a story line or even a word. I never designed my collections as an abstract statement. Whether it's the past or the present, all my ideas come from what's going on around me: from friends, music, from street culture, from memories, movies.

103 REFERENCES. It's mainly the people around me. I don't have a specific muse but I do get inspired by close friends. Leith Clark is someone that I totally admire for her effortless style. She has a childlike innocence on one hand and such passionate discipline on the other hand. She is one of the rare people that keep them both in balance without making a big deal out of it. She has a true, genuine style.

104 DEVELOPING A COLLECTION. Fashion is a tool to communicate my true self. It's

almost a visual language that enables you to communicate without using actual words. Even though my initial ideas come before practical considerations, during the process of creating I use various tools such as padding, cutting, lining, interfacing, boning, and other numerous construction techniques to build gowns that transform women into visions of elegance. It's spontaneous because it reflects what I think, who I am, and how I live.

105 MATERIALS. Fabric becomes very important in the process of translating ideas into actual garments. Fabric choice can make or break a garment, therefore it needs so much personal consideration. Fabric choice ultimately influences my designs. The drape, texture, color–these are all helpful in molding my ideas. Then the designs are generally altered and manipulated by additional draping. Each fabric works differently under the needle, each pleat or ruffle falls a certain way depending on how you drape it on the dress form.

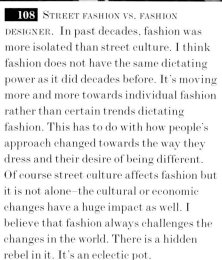

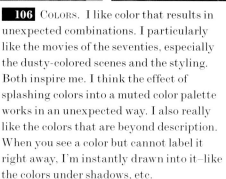

106 COLORS. I like color that results in unexpected combinations. I particularly like the movies of the seventies, especially the dusty-colored scenes and the styling. Both inspire me. I think the effect of splashing colors into a muted color palette works in an unexpected way. I also really like the colors that are beyond description. When you see a color but cannot label it right away, I'm instantly drawn into it–like the colors under shadows, etc.

107 STYLE. With fluid materials, I create three-dimensional structures that define my creativity and my own path. I have numerous convictions and seek difficult answers based on body, cloth, and the space between and around them. My aim in design is to be a perfectionist, which requires tireless efforts on improving a design many times over. For me, the ability to cut the cloth and produce abstract and complex shapes brought to life through experimentation and imagination is what my design language is based on. My ability to drape cloth, at times directly on a person, also resulted in accidental design ideas, which is at the heart of some of my most important work.

108 STREET FASHION VS. FASHION DESIGNER. In past decades, fashion was more isolated than street culture. I think fashion does not have the same dictating power as it did decades before. It's moving more and more towards individual fashion rather than certain trends dictating fashion. This has to do with how people's approach changed towards the way they dress and their desire of being different. Of course street culture affects fashion but it is not alone–the cultural or economic changes have a huge impact as well. I believe that fashion always challenges the changes in the world. There is a hidden rebel in it. It's an eclectic pot.

109 ADVICE. The best lesson is to know who you actually are as a designer. Knowing your true design identity and being loyal to it is something essential in your fashion path.

110 GOOD HABITS. A designer needs to be totally in love with what he is doing.

011

Bora Aksu
www.boraaksu.com

London-based Turkish designer, Bora Aksu received his first acclaim when he graduated from the prestigious Central Saint Martins MA course in 2002. Quoted as "the star of the show" by broadsheets such as *The Independent*, *The Daily Telegraph*, and *The Guardian*, Aksu's collection attracted not just the press but Domenico Dolce and Stefano Gabbana, who purchased pieces as inspirational items for themselves. His collaborations are varied: Via Bus Stop group, Converse, and leading London contemporary dance company Cathy Marston Project, among others. Aksu's dresses continue to woo fans including Keira Knightley, Sienna Miller, Kirsten Dunst, and Liz Jagger. With more than 10 collections under his belt, he is still amped and motivated to innovate and renovate his refined style.

012

Bruce Montgomery
www.daks.com

As menswear design director, Bruce Montgomery has been for 12 years the man behind DAKS's style, one of Britain's major fashion companies. Born and bred in Scotland, he obtained a BA (Hons) degree in fashion from the University of Northumbria. After a successful start as a designer for Nigel Cabourn, he went on to work for Katherine Hamnett in London, Luciano Soprani, Moschino, and House of Kashiyama in Milan. On his return to London in 1993, he worked as menswear designer for Jeff Banks, before joining DAKS in 1996. Aside from his work, Bruce has been appointed as vice chairman of the British Menswear Guild committee, chairman of a mentoring panel for Graduate Fashion Week, and is also an external examiner for the BA (Hons) Menswear option for the prestigious Central Saint Martins College.

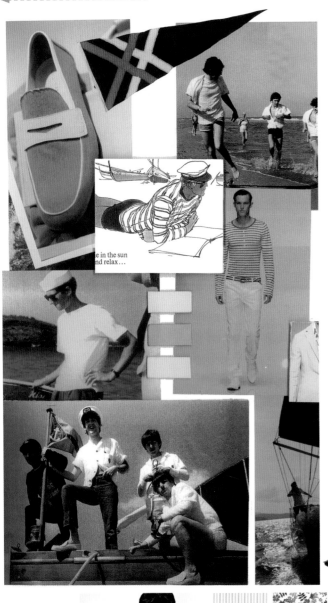

111 INSPIRATION. The theme tends to be British, and helps to focus the collection.

112 DEVELOPING A COLLECTION. I translate the concept of the collection to each item through color, styling details, and fabrication.

113 TAILORING. A balance of tradition and experimentation provides a classical reference and direction. Key items help buyers to focus the range within stores without losing the image.

114 BRAND VALUES. The collections represent a British style, that can be adapted by an individual.

115
MATERIALS. The fabrics are choosen both for visual appeal and function. They are bought from British and European fabric mills. I would stay clear of cheap polyesters.

116 COMMUNICATION. DAKS is British luxury menswear that is essentially timeless and high quality, but has a contemporary feel.

117 EVOLUTION. A designer is always looking to improve and evolve.

118 SREET FASHION VS. FASHION DESIGNER. I can not say that fashion comes from the street or from a designer proposal: it comes from all aspects of life.

119 GOOD HABITS. Collect, absorb, reject, and use.

120 SALES. It's necessary to think of the consumer wearing the garment when designing.

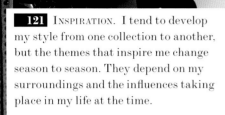

121 INSPIRATION. I tend to develop my style from one collection to another, but the themes that inspire me change season to season. They depend on my surroundings and the influences taking place in my life at the time.

122 DEVELOPING A COLLECTION. It could be translated through colors, trims, cut, and fabrics. But it should never be "heavily" translated; the concept must always remain as just that–a foundation.

123 TRADITIONAL MANUFACTURING VS. EXPERIMENTATION. Tradition and experimentation are in some ways linked. My favorite item is the jacket. The proportion is roughly the same but they are constantly under development and therefore different each time.

124 INDIVIDUALITY VS. GROUP BELONGING. The collection has to invoke individuality, it's more interesting.

125
MATERIALS. I like a smooth finish to a fabric, one with a high crease tolerance–a weight that is not too heavy with some pattern. I hate linen! It creases far too much.

126 BRAND VALUES. Quality and fit. The foundation is a strong, modern, and sexy woman. The most challenging thing is to be constant.

127 COMMUNICATION. Communication is key to success. My team and I make sure we are always in tune with each area of the business. Design, sales, and PR are all linked and one cannot work without the other.

128 STREET FASHION VS. FASHION DESIGNER. I would say both.

129 ADVICE. Central Saint Martins was the best lesson in every sense. Go there! Work, work, and more work.

130 SALES. What works for sales does not always work for catwalk and press. I have to maintain a balance between the two while not creating pieces that dilute my signature.

013

Bryce d'Anicé Aime
www.bryce-danice-aime.com

Originally from France, Bryce d'Anicé Aime came to London in 1998 and cultivated his talent at Central Saint Martins where he graduated with a BA Honors in 2005. D'Anicé launched his eponymous label the following year, presenting a highly successful debut collection for S/S 07.

D'Anicé Aime's central inspiration is taken from the arts, architecture, and philosophy. His designs reflect an intriguing mix of form, function, and finish, providing an ongoing foundation for each collection. His clothes are created for the woman who recognizes the understated appeal

of luxurious fabrics, elegant cuts, and precise finishes to create a distinct yet quiet drama within her wardrobe. Bryce d'Anicé Aime offers a made-to-measure demi-couture service from his Holland Park studio for clients who enjoy a totally personal experience.

© Carlota Santamaria

014

Carlota Santamaria, Susana Del Sol/just4fun
www.just4funweb.com

This is a design studio involved in different areas of fashion: fashion design, coolhunting, fashion journalism, and photography. Its purpose is to create a fashion project not restricted by conventional fashion industry standards, like seasons and large-scale manufacturing; and the results are unique and original pieces. They are in collaboration with small local workshops and a female prisoners rehabilitation center who produce leggings, jumpsuits, and tube skirts from fabrics that the just4fun team chooses personally in stores around their home city of Barcelona, or on trips to Paris, New York, Tokyo, or any market in any part of the world.

131 INSPIRATION. The start of just4fun was a line of basics differentiated by their prints and limited editions. The choice of fabrics would be our link with inspiration, which comes from our feelings and passions.

132 DEVELOPMENT OF A COLLECTION. We don't work with a concept for our collection, as they tend to do in fashion. We have one basic and permanent concept: unique pieces, regardless of the season. The most important principle is to put into practice our Social Care Manufacturing system. Everything is 100% made in Barcelona by very specialist workers in small local workshops involved in a program for the social rehabilitation of ex-prisoners. We like to think that the person using our clothes feels like they are a part of a common project.

133 YOUR RIGHT ARM? Being a twosome, we rely on each other for everything. The idea came from both of us. It was a fusion between the one's passion for leggings and the other's taste for prints. Both of us know clearly what the brand means and we mutually support each other.

134 BRAND VALUES. We do limited editions and fun prints that show solidarity. We believe that that is enough to make you feel different when you use just4fun. You're part of a project that disassociates itself from the conventional fashion system.

© Carlota Santamaria

135 MATERIALS. We choose stretch fabrics because our pieces are fitted. We choose them one by one, and we search the world for special prints. It's easy to lose track and the next minute you're imagining its movement on a leg; you get excited and can't wait to have it made so you can wear it. Prints change a lot when you make them up. It's not the same to see it as a 1-meter length and to then see it as leggings with a 25-centimeter leg measurement. The sketch is different; and that's a point to keep in mind.

© Carlota Santamaria

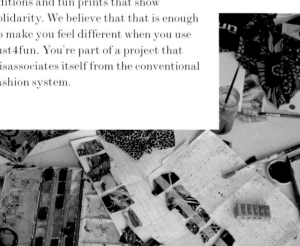

© Carlota Santamaria

© Carlota Santamaria

© Carlota Santamaria

136 COMMUNICATION. We choose the Internet as our means of exposure and sell through e-commerce. Focusing on an online presence gives us total freedom and control over our image. Basing our project on a website means we achieve a very important goal for us: the democratization of our label. It doesn't matter where in the world you're from, if you have access to the Internet, you can see our new designs and you can buy what you like most—we send it to you wherever you are.

137 IMAGE. From the very beginning we clearly knew that we wanted a simple, strong, and contemporary image. We decided on a black and white logo in textspeak and in a classic font. Our image in advertising campaigns and catalogs is based on a photo over a white background to enhance the piece. We don't want forced or provocative attitudes; the models have their own personalities, just like our customers.

138 STREET FASHION VS. FASHION DESIGNER. Fashion comes from the street. Designers, like the rest, experience a certain time, they take in an artistic climate, and are influenced by social, economic, political, and cultural margins, just like everybody else. But designers work like catalysts for all these influences and turn them into a design that can belong to or be on the sidelines of a "trend."

139 GOOD HABITS. Work, work, and work.

140 SALES. Whenever someone buys something from just4fun, we feel that someone new has joined the project. I don't think we've ever stopped being excited. It makes us proud to see our brand in the street, in a magazine, out dancing... wherever, as long as it's alive!

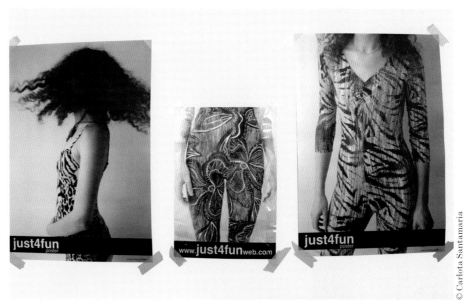

© Carlota Santamaria

© Carlota Santamaria

© Carlota Santamaria

© Carlota Santamaria

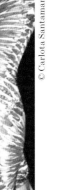

© Carlota Santamaria

141 INSPIRATION. The creation of a trend directory is very important. You have to create a new point of view; the people need new dreams, new emotions. Don't be afraid to create a new vision of fashion.

142 REFERENCES. When I start a collection my first thought is "what face does this woman have?" and "what is her history?" I design her face and later I think about lines, color, and fabric.

143 WORKPLACE. I need to design in a systematic chaos. All ideas are mixed in a "no sense taste." You can take inspiration from a retro photo or a chocolate paper. In my house I love to design in my kitchen or in my bed.

144 STYLE. My style is pop. Translating the concept is easy because I don't adapt the concept by the lines of the clothes, but it is the dress that is completely transformed to represent the themes. Pop, that's all!

145 INDIVIDUALITY VS. GROUP BELONGING. Fiorucci is a streetwear brand, so underground culture belongs to its history, no place for individuality.

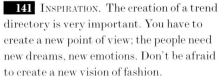

THIS COLLECTION WAS CALLED "love army", as you can see the love inspiration is evidet!!

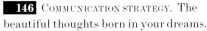

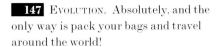

146 COMMUNICATION STRATEGY. The beautiful thoughts born in your dreams.

147 EVOLUTION. Absolutely, and the only way is pack your bags and travel around the world!

148 IS FASHION ART? If you design for a commercial brand then you don't make art—you have to create nice clothes that people can easily wear. In my private life, I love to make illustrations and paintings. At the end, I think true art can't exist in commercial marketing.

this is me working in my first team..in front of me my two friends :

Mary (product manager)
Alice (senior designer)

149 ADVICE. I have learned the best lesson during my first job experience. I was designing with two girls that passed on the secret to me: working in teams is the key to success! Remember that if you want to make something all by yourself, you'll make bad work.

150

GOOD HABITS. I can say what a designer doesn't have to do: don't go to hipster parties, don't feel like a superstar, don't be a victim of the fashion system, create your own style.

015

Carlotta Costanzo/Fiorucci
www.fiorucci.it

One of the pioneer Italian brands, the Fiorucci label was founded by Elio Fiorucci in 1967. Its original intent was to bring the latest trends from the Swinging London and American classics, such as the T-shirt and jeans, to a then burgeoning Italian fashion scene. By the late seventies and early eighties the company had made a strong trendsetting name for itself especially in the US. Those were the days of the so-called daytime Studio 54, attracting such scenesters as Andy Warhol to a young Madonna. The label never failed to be on the crest of the wave, introducing iconic eighties must-haves such as camouflage prints and leopard-skin prints. Carlotta Costanzo is a young Italian designer. After a period at Luciano Soprani, she joined Fiorucci, bringing her energy and creative flair as a senior designer.

016

Carolin Lerch/Pelican Avenue
www.pelicanavenue.com

Carolin Lerch runs the label Pelican Avenue. Lerch was born in Austria and moved to Belgium in 1995 to study fashion at the Royal Academy of Fine Arts in Antwerp. After working for Bernhard Willhelm, she established her own label in 2004 to question the conventional codes of fashion and oppose the constantly changing trends of the Western fashion industry. Consequently, she elaborates on her projects through a wide range of media, from photography and video to installation and performance. She also works together with multimedia artist Michiel Helbig using their common platform–Pelican Video. Her way of crossing over different fields gives her collections a distinct approach, parallel to contemporary art, while retaining meaning and clearly conveying a message in each project.

© Pelican Video

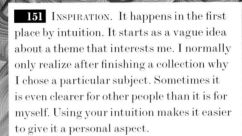

© Bettina Komenda

151 INSPIRATION. It happens in the first place by intuition. It starts as a vague idea about a theme that interests me. I normally only realize after finishing a collection why I chose a particular subject. Sometimes it is even clearer for other people than it is for myself. Using your intuition makes it easier to give it a personal aspect.

152 MATERIALS. For me, the fabric is the very start of the collection, when I begin to think about the actual pieces of clothing. It determines the shapes more than the shapes determine the fabric. Going through fabric swatches is an inspiring process that has a lot to do with the craft of a designer.

153 DEVELOPING A COLLECTION. The shapes are a rather emotional and personal expression of a creative language for me. The concept and the image are a subconscious process based on a personal experience, whereas the fabric choice is the knowledge–the professional back catalogue.

The more you know about clothes and work with them, the easier it will get and the less mistakes you will make.

154 YOUR RIGHT ARM? My boyfriend and partner in our video platform Pelican Video. On the one hand, he is my most honest critic, but on the other hand his enthusiasm helps me through difficult periods. Besides, our common videos gave Pelican Avenue its own way to express fashion, its own identity.

155 BRAND VALUES. I wanted to keep possibilities more open by not using my own name. I always liked synonyms because they have a certain mystery and Pelican Avenue (the street I live and used to work on) has the feel of a lost glory. It's misleading because it has something conservative, which it isn't at all! I like the confusion it brings up.

© Pelican Video

© Biel Sol

157 STYLE. I can not seem to get rid of a certain simplicity in shapes. Even though this is not totally a conscious choice, I still avoid cuts and detailing that seems unnecessary. Materials, colors, and motives are things I tend to get fed up with from time to time. It is the conscious choices that change rather than the personal artistic language that is developed instinctively.

158 STREET FASHION VS. FASHION DESIGNER. I think there used to be clear development coming from the street, maybe until the eighties. Nowadays what we find in stores is more influenced by a commercial and economic masterplan than we realize. Of course, there is a group of high fashion designers that succeed in staying independent.

159 ADVICE. You can't become someone you are not. It's better to accept this as soon as possible and start making the best of it.

160 GOOD HABITS. Fantasy and open-mindness, self-criticism, endurance, and self-assertion.

156
EVOLUTION. I believe that improvement is nothing to worry about. It's a natural thing that happens when you concentrate and continue to work consciously. It has something to do with getting more and more professional. What is more difficult is to succeed combining this craft with an innovative strength.

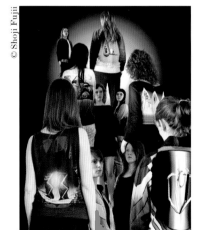

© Shoji Fujii

©Tabassom Charaf

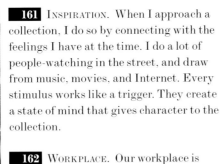

161 INSPIRATION. When I approach a collection, I do so by connecting with the feelings I have at the time. I do a lot of people-watching in the street, and draw from music, movies, and Internet. Every stimulus works like a trigger. They create a state of mind that gives character to the collection.

162 WORKPLACE. Our workplace is extremely chaotic. The table I share with my team is full of magazines, color swatches, prototypes, cookies, and cups of coffee. I believe it reflects the way we take our work, as an integral part of our lives because ideas don't only come from our table, sometimes they occur to us at home, when talking to friends, and in any other situation. And likewise, things come into the office that do not strictly belong to the world of design.

163 MATERIALS. We mainly work with leather, which we buy from local tanneries. We interact with them a great deal in regard to seasonal developments (more or less shine, aged or wrinkled leathers...). We order our own colors; in other words we design our own range practically from scratch. Color is absolutely fundamental in our collections. We are quite daring

compared to the normal leather goods market, which tends to go for safe colors (black, brown, and tan). We like to play with color because it totally changes the concept of each collection and gives it personality.

164 BRAND VALUES. The Jet concept offers modernity, style that goes beyond what is trendy, and extremely high quality. In its beginnings, the brand was inspired by leather travel goods from the fifties, when traveling was a glamorous event. This glamour was combined with research into materials which produced results such as the use of neoprene and punched leather. A great deal of work also went into function, both in use and in adapting pieces to the body. These concepts are taken up again each season and new ones are added, examples of which could be futurism, retro, or any other theme of interest to us at the time, but always translated into Jet's language.

165 IS FASHION ART? I don't believe design is art. It shares art's search for the creation of beautiful things, and the particular contribution of those creating it (the designer's "eye" and approach).

166 INDIVIDUALITY VS. GROUP BELONGING. Fashion is exclusivity in the sense that I can choose what I want for me and use it in my own particular way. And it is democratization because trends are expressed on all levels and it is possible to dress in a similar way; in other words, to communicate a similar message about oneself, but within the limitation of widely differing budgets.

167 TRAINING. The best lesson I learned is that one should have fun, question oneself, and experience work as a challenge; in short, not resorting to the obvious to find solutions.

168 GOOD HABITS. Designers should be up to date with everything. They should observe and observe. Try, think, and laugh (also at one's self and what one is doing).

169 SALES. A collection sells well when it's in tune with the vibes of the season, when it offers what clients want in terms of function, and when it becomes desirable. When I think of a collection, I think of what I would like to wear and what our clients would like to find, what will entice them. Added to this is the goal of creating an original, personal, and beautiful design.

170 ACKNOWLEDGEMENT. The best reward is to see a product of mine in the street being used with style, combined in a way that I wouldn't have imagined, and taking on a life of its own.

017

Carolina Ainstein/Lazaro, Jet
www.lazarocuero.com.ar

Some 60 years ago, the Nielawicky brothers of Argentina set up a family business producing leather gloves and belts, making use of the excellent hides produced there. The high quality of their products along with their exquisite finishing (at a level comparable to handcrafted pieces instead of manufactured goods) was good publicity for the company, which shortly after became the local market leader. With this background and years of experience in the field, the younger generation of the family decided to start up a new brand in the early eighties that would uphold the standards of quality they were accustomed to, while diversifying their products. Their brand, Lazaro, offers leather wallets and purses, accessories, and garments, with first-class design.

018

Céline Kamara-Gouge/Touch Luxe
www.touchluxe.eu

Céline Kamara-Gouge, one of Touch Luxe's founding members, bases her collections on a model of femininity that presents audacity, readiness, and contemporaneousness. Formed at the Duperré School of Arts of Paris, along with Patricia Forgeal and Franck Albou, Céline had in mind to transfer a style to fashion that wouldn't obey any rules. Designing for today's city girls, all of the items sport adorned noble fabrics and playful finishes for a style that embodies the term "sexy casual." This approach has contributed to their success and their garments have been featured in many major fashion magazines. Among her influences we find such diverse figures as Katy Perry, Liv Taylor, Kelis, Asia Argento, Laura Smet, and Michelle Obama.

171 INSPIRATION. The departure point of a collection is most of the time chosen at random. It can result from a simple thought in time or just from the sight of a passerby who inspires me and makes the link between all the elements I already had in mind. I already know the guiding lines for the next summer collection theme thanks to a detail on a pair of customized jeans I saw on a guy during a Paris night out.

172 MUSES. When I design I systematically think of two type of women. On one hand, I think of my own friends: young city women in their thirties who represent through their diversity the brand's clientele. On the other, I think of those I call my "icons," female artists whom I admire both their work and their looks. I rarely think of myself when I am drawing.

173
DEVELOPING A COLLECTION. You have to see it in its entirety, whether through a catwalk, in a flagship store, or in a commercial show room. A garment taken out of its context simply becomes a cute sweater or a beautiful dress. The truth is that each garment echoes another piece of the collection while the references and all-over patterns underline the main themes.

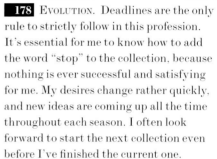

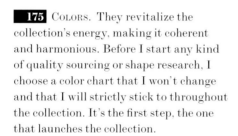

174 MATERIALS. I'm in search of singularity. When I travel, I spend time in local markets looking for rare garments or vintage fabrics related to my initial idea. I also do sourcing during professional fabric manufacturers' fairs where I favor quality, Italian weavers or French embroiderers' know-how for the luxurious part of the brand. I work with Asian manufacturers who exclusively develop prints for each collection.

175 COLORS. They revitalize the collection's energy, making it coherent and harmonious. Before I start any kind of quality sourcing or shape research, I choose a color chart that I won't change and that I will strictly stick to throughout the collection. It's the first step, the one that launches the collection.

176 BRAND VALUES. Touch Luxe offers a line with noble materials and haute couture details that simultaneously plays with the actual trends and cuts–what the trendy girls want today. Customers come to find the atypical detail, the opposite of basic, slightly rebel. They like claiming and playing with their freedom in fashion, while remainig refined and feminine.

177 COMMUNICATION. Our message is to never follow any rules, to follow your favorites, and to not be taken too seriously. Our clothes are like fetishes, objects of desire; women become their own Barbie.

178 EVOLUTION. Deadlines are the only rule to strictly follow in this profession. It's essential for me to know how to add the word "stop" to the collection, because nothing is ever successful and satisfying for me. My desires change rather quickly, and new ideas are coming up all the time throughout each season. I often look forward to start the next collection even before I've finished the current one.

179 IS FASHION ART? I do not make art, for sure. I make clothes to express my internal matter, but at the end of the day they are still just garments.

180 GOOD HABITS. A designer should have some good quality pumps for all travels and a very big bag because, if you are messy like me, you accumulate a ton of things while shopping–like sketch books, a camera, magazines, iPod, cell phone, diary, and many fabrics–that you end up carrying around with you all day. Today's essential for me is the basic grey, hooded zipper sweatshirt that I wear with my Touch Luxe dresses in a relaxed and cool way.

181

REFERENCES. The most important thing is to design clothes that people want to wear. It is easy to overcomplicate designs. We focus on clean lines and interesting, wearable silhouettes.

182 INSPIRATION. Each Limedrop collection has an overall theme and title that have to reflect the fun nature of Limedrop. Themes are definitely a strong part of our brand identy. S/S 08 "All 3 Dimensions" collection lookbook was photographed in stereo (where you can view the campaign with 3D glasses) and had a color palette of red, cyan, silver, white, and black. S/S 09 "Snakes and Ladders" collection came with a board game.

183 MATERIALS. Fabric is one of the most important parts of our products. We have over a dozen suppliers and view numerous fabric collections to choose the best for the season. We look for unique finishes and plains that we can print/treat to make our own.

184 COMMUNICATION. Our message is young and fresh. We try to position the brand in events that take an innovative approach to showcasing fashion. We held a live photo shoot event as part of Penthouse Mouse pop-up retail store and L'Oréal Melbourne Fashion Festival. The audience was able to see a Limedrop fashion photo shoot in progress and witness the backstage. Limedrop promises fun, energy, and imagination.

185 EVOLUTION. If you stagnate you will be left behind. There is a fine line between offering a signature range of products and repeating the same thoughts. Each season we change our key looks and still reinvent styles from the previous one, so that there is a connection and story. We want people to incorporate what's new into their wardrobe, and not completely start over again each season.

© Tom Friml/www.tomasfriml.com

© Hubert van Doorn

© Jo Duck/www.joduck.com

© Anna Marcella

© Mia Mala McDonald/www.miamalamcdonald.com

© Jo Duck/www.joduck.com

186 STYLE. We would like to think that our style improves and strengthens with each collection. As designers, we are learning and refining, but as this learning process happens there are some mistakes that will live in peoples' minds. It is a risky business.

187 SREET FASHION VS. FASHION DESIGNER. Fashion comes from the clothes people wear and desire to wear. Designers are the people who bring that to life–there are always new ideas.

188 GOOD HABITS. A designer should have the desire to challenge and question everything, and the innate need to learn more.

189 SALES. They result from a mix of quality product, timing, and good PR. Good sales are the only way we are able to continue the brand, so it definitely influences our creativity. We have to juggle what we would like to design and what people want to buy. Creativity for us cannot be a self-indulgent pursuit, nor can it be all about the end result. There must be balance.

190 ACKNOWLEDGEMENT. Limedrop is best praised for our ability to offer the unexpected and not take ourselves too seriously.

019

Clea Garrick, Nathan Price/Limedrop
www.limedrop.com.au

Clea Garrick and Nathan Price are the minds behind Limedrop, an Australian fashion label that captures the imagination and the spirit of possibilities. The fashion label is made up of a collection of men's and ladies' clothing and wooden accessories. Limedrop fashion is known for its use of clear lines, bold colors, structured pieces, and curious proportions. The design duo is always coming up with new ideas and the response from buyers and the public has been strong. From humble beginnings as a rucksack bursting with designs to delivering their fifth collection "Snakes and Ladders" in both the northern and southern hemisphere for spring/ summer. The label has set a strong base in the Australian market while international buyers are embracing their fresh designs with open arms.

020

Cora Groppo
www.coragroppo.com

Cora Groppo was born in Argentina in 1971 and studied fashion design at the University of Buenos Aires. After working for well-known Argentinean labels like Vitamina and Yagmour, she started her own, Coragroppo, in 1987. At first, she sold haute couture gowns and wedding dresses.

For the past seven years, Coragroppo has presented itself as an urban fashion label with two stores in Buenos Aires. Groppo opened the first of these in Palermo Viejo six years ago and the second, in the Recoleta district four years ago. Cora Groppo's collections are sold in countries such

as the US, Spain, the Netherlands, France, Britain, Indonesia, Mexico, and Chile, and have appeared as features in international publications, among them *Elle*, *Vogue*, and *Cosmopolitan*. Cora Groppo opened her first European store in Rome in 2009.

191

INSPIRATION. For me, every collection comes out of the previous one. The first step is to continue researching the last theme to find a new technique that lets me start again. My search is related with inventing a technique for construction. To find it, I do tests on a mannequin that turns and that enables me to work the body by going around it, by handling fabrics, and experimenting.

192 DEVELOPING A COLLECTION. As the concept always has something to do with one or several construction techniques, it's easier for me to apply it to other products. It is also very interesting because the different materials generally enrich the technique.

193 MATERIALS. I'm not biased. I like to try out new things. I am very demanding with quality–not only with the raw materials, but also with how the fabric is made. I like noble fabrics, generally with Lycra. I also like to work with knitted fabrics. Fabrics inspire me.

194 COLORS. I generally choose the same colors. I very much like and am interested in working with single colors in one garment, only changing the nature of the material. I don't like strong colors, and those that are "in" even less. I have my own palette of grays, beiges, naturals, blues, blacks, and browns. I don't normally work with color contrasts and I take the liberty of repeating myself on this point.

195 BRAND VALUES. Cora Groppo promises intellectuality.

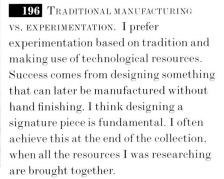

196 TRADITIONAL MANUFACTURING VS. EXPERIMENTATION. I prefer experimentation based on tradition and making use of technological resources. Success comes from designing something that can later be manufactured without hand finishing. I think designing a signature piece is fundamental. I often achieve this at the end of the collection, when all the resources I was researching are brought together.

197 COMMUNICATION. I am personally in charge of publicity. I'm not particularly interested in knowing a lot about the rules of marketing. I've come to realize that the most important thing is the product. It has to be able to communicate everything you think. At the heart of things, my form of publicity is the tool for expressing ourselves. I'm not trying to convey premeditated messages.

198 EVOLUTION. I feel that I have to push myself to excel every six months. It's incredible how untiring it can be. Confidence and consistency are two basic rules for building up a creative space and for putting a team together that identifies with the project.

199 STYLE. With time, I've come to understand how important it is to hold on to certain things without losing the ability to surprise, which isn't easy. In order to create an identity, you have to keep working on certain elements that interest you, such as the palette, the study of morphology, textures, and proportions.

200 ACKNOWLEDGEMENT. Whereas the five minutes of glory during the runway show are pure adrenalin, the real approval or genuine success is in a product that is irresistible to clients, and that they finally end up choosing to buy.

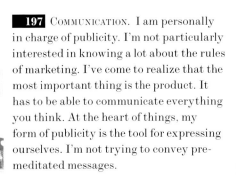

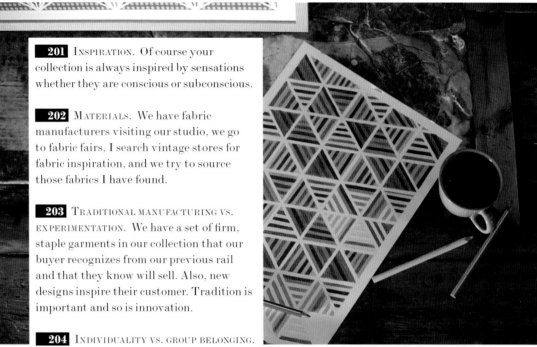

201 INSPIRATION. Of course your collection is always inspired by sensations whether they are conscious or subconscious.

202 MATERIALS. We have fabric manufacturers visiting our studio, we go to fabric fairs, I search vintage stores for fabric inspiration, and we try to source those fabrics I have found.

203 TRADITIONAL MANUFACTURING VS. EXPERIMENTATION. We have a set of firm, staple garments in our collection that our buyer recognizes from our previous rail and that they know will sell. Also, new designs inspire their customer. Tradition is important and so is innovation.

204 INDIVIDUALITY VS. GROUP BELONGING. Individuality I guess. I hope that with the colors I use, those who wear my garments will stand out.

205 BRAND VALUES. Youthfulness, zest, fun.

© Linda Brownlee

© Linda Brownlee

© Toyin

© Linda Brownlee

206 IS FASHION ART? I am an artist working in fashion.

207 ADVICE. Don't spend loads of money until you know you've got a return; don't take a gamble if you don't have a backup.

208 SALES. If you've got no bucks you will come across many hurdles. I didn't think I was running a business in the beginning. It's easy to jump on the rollercoaster of creativity and spend, spend, spend, but you will sink like a heavy ship if you don't make money. Always be prepared to not make any money because fashion is expensive and the return can be just the opposite. It is a business and you can never afford to forget that.

209 ACKNOWLEDGEMENT. It's the American *Vogue* and British *Vogue* four-page spreads in the same month.

©Toyin

©Toyin

210

GOOD HABITS. Brush your teeth, be good to your peers, don't make it a competition, and don't compare yourself to others–it could be your downfall. And a secret: if you're not a bitch in fashion you will stand out.

© Linda Brownlee

021

David Saunders/David David
www.daviddavid.co.uk

English designer David Saunders launched his label David David in 2004 after years of experience in the art world where he had the opportunity to work with outstanding artists, Tracey Emin among them. When he started out in fashion, David made highly detailed and hand-printed patterned T-shirts, with each one looking as if it were a new work of art. This quickly brought him to the attention of the press and buyers. Today his geometric prints have become his signature look. He has expanded his line to complete prêt-à-porter collections that he presents each season at London Fashion Week, and which are sold in famous stores the world over, among them Colette in Paris, Seven in New York, Edition in Japan, and Dover Street Market and Harvey Nichols in London.

022

Delphine Papiernik/Kickers
www.kickers.com

Early in 1970, Daniel Raufast came across a billboard showing a picture of teenagers dressed in colorful T-shirts and jeans, but not one of them was wearing any shoes. His mind was made up; he had to create a new design of shoe that could be worn with jeans for this laid-back generation. That is how Kickers and its legendary ankle boot came into being. Created in 1970, the Kickers shoe was born from the imagination of its founder back then, chairman of E. Raufast & Sons, a company that specialized in luxury shoes for children. Daniel shared his idea with friend designer Jacques Chevallereau. Soon enough, the two had come up with what became the trademark boot of their collection, helping the brand successfully deploy first in France and then in the rest of the world.

211 INSPIRATION. Trends are everywhere–in a book, on a runway, in a boutique, and in cosmetics. The first thing I do is research a general idea that is repeated in different settings; I observe it as a sociological trend for a specific time.

212 REFERENCES. We identify a mother trend some two years earlier, one that will be the brand strategy to be followed in that collection. We then choose colors, we decide on product diversification, and plan the opening of new retail outlets.

213 DEVELOPING A COLLECTION. There's no single idea in each season; there are main concepts that have to be in all of the products. Some of these ideas are not fashion. They're brand values and, as such, are timeless. They always have to be present in every one of our lines–men, women, and children–but worked in a different way in each of them.

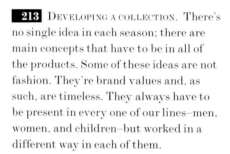

214 MANUFACTURING. When we design a collection, we respect our code: Kickers is an authentic, *decontracté*, casual brand. Topstitch detail is one of our hallmarks, because we respect the essence of the original shoe in its manufacture and in its sole. Our origins were inspired by jeans and we convey this informal language in the production of footwear.

215 BRAND VALUES. When making footwear, quality and comfort are basics. The promise of the brand is a reliable and stylish shoe.

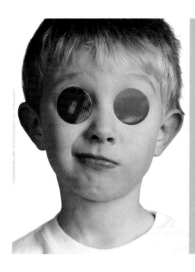

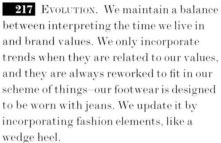

RED LEFT,
GREEN RIGHT

217 EVOLUTION. We maintain a balance between interpreting the time we live in and brand values. We only incorporate trends when they are related to our values, and they are always reworked to fit in our scheme of things—our footwear is designed to be worn with jeans. We update it by incorporating fashion elements, like a wedge heel.

218 STYLE. We work with a guiding thread for the collection that is shared by all of the departments: production, sales, PR, and marketing.

219 COMMUNICATION. We need to position ourselves as a "transgenerational" brand, and to achieve this we have 360-degree publicity: institutions, press relations, product launches, marketing actions, fashion publications, etc.

220 SALES. Our main market is children, and by extension, the adults who share their world. Our customers don't have any specific age but they do have an attitude towards life: to play and have fun together with children. Grown-ups love Kickers because they are reminded of their childhood.

216
TEAMWORK. In our atelier we have a notice board where the members of the team attach their ideas. There, we can see things ranging from a collage with a color palette to secondary ideas. Then we choose the ideas that we materialize.

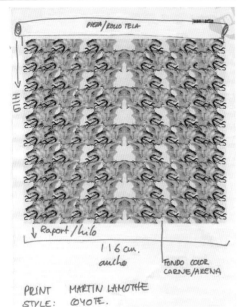

PIEZA / ROLLO TELA

Raport / hilo

116 cm. ancho

FONDO COLOR CARNE/ARENA

PRINT STYLE: MARTIN LAMOTHE COYOTE.

221 INSPIRATION. When I start to design, I think of feelings, especially the ones conjured up by a view, a landscape. I don't have anyone particular in mind while I'm designing, though I do have colors, characters, and even phrases and music.

222 DEVELOPING A COLLECTION. I have several test dummies and I use one or the other depending on whether I need to see the whole piece or just sort out problems with a part. In order to transmit the idea of the collection to each garment and accessory, I'll sometimes use patternmaking and at other times I'll use the fabric; however, it's almost the balance of the two that makes it work. I want the concept to be recognized without it being a disguise.

© Nacho Alegre

223 TRADITIONAL MANUFACTURING VS. EXPERIMENTATION. Whether or not it's a good thing, you tend to create a signature piece. In my case it's the cape; it's my color palette for the collection. I prefer experimentation, but I do it through fabrics and not so much through shapes.

224 INDIVIDUALITY VS. GROUP BELONGING. My clothes make people feel different; although if they were all together, they would be the Martin Lamothe tribe, which has happened one time or another. The label promises color, concept, and looks, obviously!

225

MATERIALS. I choose a cloth because I fall in love with the feeling it gives me or because of the possibilities it has. I often buy them and later I manipulate them so much that not even the manufacturer can identify them. They tend to be local or European manufacturers. I look for a lot in each color–my vision depends on them. Most of the time I make my own colors so that they harmonize with my prints.

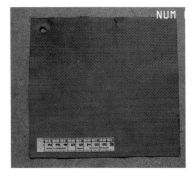

226 COMMUNICATION. I place so much importance on it, so much so that Martin Lamothe has its own press people, led by Victoria Gómez. Our message is clear and underground: it's art and music. Our strategy is to work with nationally- and internationally-known artists to complete the concept of the collections. We do this as a whole and cover everything, including photos, objects, and even video art.

227 EVOLUTION. It isn't a case of outdoing yourself every season; it's progressing or giving as much of yourself as the last. I feel like I'm evolving. I'm maturing and leaving behind easy solutions so I can learn to express myself more in my own way and less in a way that's distant from what I mean.

228 IS FASHION ART? I don't do art. I do fashion, but I do it creatively. A small part of fashion is born in the street and another part comes from designers. It's like a virtuous circle.

229 GOOD HABITS. The best attitude to have is to think that everything can always be better. A designer's work has to be demanding and not at all complacent. The best prize is when you see the collection comes together at the pre-show fitting.

230 SALES. In terms of independent fashion, I haven't managed to find out what the secret to good sales is, because suddenly one piece you think is impossible sells heaps, while a more commercial piece doesn't sell at all. So I leave analysis aside and try to make the collection as pretty as I can. If you excite, you sell. Of course, that only works if prices don't go over the top.

© Hugo de la Rosa

© Biel Sol

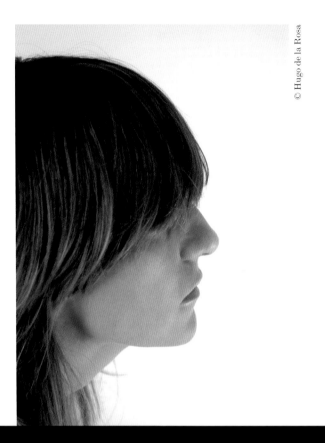

© Hugo de la Rosa

023

Elena Martín/Martin Lamothe
www.martinlamothe.es

Martin Lamothe, started in 2006, is the label of Barcelona designer Elena Martín. Drawn to fashion and architecture, Elena Martín graduated with a degree in fashion design in Barcelona and, at the age of 20, was the youngest student to be admitted to Central Saint Martins College in London, where she completed a master's degree in fashion. After working for Markus Constable and RL, she collaborated with Mr. Jones as a stylist for such stars as Howie B. and Kylie Minogue, and became director of design for Antonio Miró's diffusion label, Miro Jeans. Elena Martín launched Martin Lamothe Goes Unisex as a unisex prêt-à-porter line after the success of her designs for men. Martin Lamothe collections are currently sold in Australia, Japan, Korea, the US, and Europe.

024 Estrella Archs
www.estrellaarchs.com

After graduating with honors from the prestigious Central Saint Martins College of Arts and Design in London, Catalan designer Estrella Archs was given the opportunity to travel and work for the leading firms in the world of fashion, such as Hussein Chalayan in London, Nina Ricci and Cacharel in Paris, Emilio Pucci for Christian Lacroix in Florence, and Prada in Milan, before setting up her own label. Estrella's designs combine new and clean forms with a highly developed sense of femininity, sensuality, and poetry. Their apparent simplicity is the expression of an art that intensifies the qualities of a woman and the impact she leaves wherever she goes. Her delicate pieces can be found in boutiques in Paris, Barcelona, and Kuwait.

231 INSPIRATION. My inspiration comes from today's women and their lives, along with sunsets, starry skies, silence, the wind, children, saints, and mad people.

232 WORKPLACE. Emilia is my mannequin; she has nearly always traveled with me on every occasion. I like to work in a detached and harmonious atmosphere; my studio is like a dance school. My drawing table is somewhat rustic, a stone slab, and everything I need at a given moment is on it.

233 REFERENCES. I think of active women in the world who are aware of their lives, women with a sense of humor and elegance, sensitivity and sobriety, who are surprising and discreet.

234 DEVELOPING A COLLECTION. Depending on the tone of the collection, I can do it straight on the mannequin, with a sketch, by means of a collage, or with a suggestive splash of paint.

235 MATERIALS. I use natural fabrics, but I also use the most technically advanced Japanese fabrics. I buy cloth all over the world. It all depends on the concept of the collection at the time. Natural fabrics are magic. Their contact with the skin is amazing, and this can affect one's state of mind, smell, perspiration, and relations with others.

236
PHILOSOPHY. I feel I have to give the best of myself at all times and contribute to women's lives on a personal and social level. Being a designer is a great responsibility.

237 TRADITIONAL MANUFACTURING VS. EXPERIMENTATION. I try to design new things, but with the weight and wisdom of the classics. My signature piece is called Monade, and is an original silhouette.

238 BRAND VALUES. Being honest.

239 IS FASHION ART? I make dresses inspired by the art of living life.

240 SALES. For a collection to sell well you have to believe in it; there are no rules to define what is commercial on the market.

241 INSPIRATION. We think of themes that appeal to us, like the identities in the "Identities" collection, or the theme of changing looks in the "Mutant Beauty" collection. The latter was inspired by a television show where contestants were given a radical makeover with cosmetic surgery to make them happier. Themes are like a box of creative information where you can pull out forms, prints, colors, and illustrations. They're essential.

242 DEVELOPING A COLLECTION. I stick everything up on a huge board on the wall to see the colors, fabrics, and forms; then I design each piece one at a time.

243 MATERIALS. I choose fabrics according to the concept of the collection, what I want to convey, the weight, the form it gives...I never use very synthetic fabrics that make people feel bad.

244 TRADITIONAL MANUFACTURING VS. EXPERIMENTATION. A mixture. The best thing is to experiment starting from tradition.

245 BRAND VALUES. Fun, certain exclusivity, and being different.

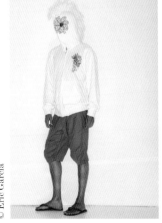

© Eric Garcia

246 REFERENCES. We often collaborate with an artist. For instance, we collaborated with Charity on our last collection. We met her at a festival called Drap Art that focused on recycled art. She has a project called Somany projects, where she takes soft toys and transforms them into something different by changing their parts, the way it's done with people. It was a simple approach to the more extreme theme of cosmetic surgery for the collection "Mutant Beauty."

247 COMMUNICATION. Communication is essential. In fact, we have a background in communication. For us, the design of a collection is communicating a message using all of its supports. When you wear a piece of clothing, you are communicating a lot about yourself: tastes in music, social status, state of mind, background, culture, etc. The image of a campaign is yet another support for communicating the concept that is transmitted through the clothes.

248 COMMUNICATION STRATEGY. The message is the theme of the collection and the strategy is channeled through the support that is considered necessary in each collection: postcards, online mailing, website, displays, and the actual labels on the garments. We have a very particular image and we intend to be faithful to it.

249 INDIVIDUALITY VS. GROUP BELONGING. Fashion is democratization or exclusivity, depending on what you are willing to pay.

250 SALES. A well-balanced collection is one made up of clothes that present an image; those that are shown on the runway and featured by the press that communicate a concept well and are innovative; and those that are more commercial—in other words, that are more wearable for a wider public.

© Núria Romero

© Eric García

© Núria Romero

025 Eva Riu, Alberto Gabari/The Mystic Onion
www.themysticonion.com

Catalan Eva Riu and native of Madrid Alberto Gabari met at ESDi, the design college in Sabadell where they both studied graphic design. After graduating, they each went their separate ways–Albert went for illustration while Eva was more interested in fashion–until three years ago, when they decided to work together and create The Mystic Onion. The collections they make are limited and exclusive, with creative, quality pieces that seek to create a link between fashion and artistic expression. In addition to their collections, they also participate in events, exhibitions, performances, and festivals. The Mystic Onion is currently distributed in a number of European countries including Spain, Italy, Belgium, and Denmark.

026

Evangelina Bomparola
www.evangelinabomparola.com

Fashion designer, journalist, historian, mother, and a figure of Argentinean society, Evangelina Bomparola is a complete and intriguing woman. She is a person who takes pleasure and amusement from clothes along with the feelings she seeks to transmit to others. This doctrine is behind the way she runs her fashion house. Starting in 2002 with private work, she later opened a showroom and now has a boutique in the Recoleta district of Buenos Aires.

She is an advocate of the casual chic that began in the 90s in Paris, and her label presents a street look combined with luxury. Her made-to-measure clothes service advises clients on everything they need, and teaches them how to enhance their figures to the best effect. For Eva, "having a dress made on your own body, with darts in the right places to flatter you, is the greatest expression of luxury."

251 INSPIRATION. There can be one trigger or many. My travels are my most important source of inspiration; although inspiration can also come from an art exhibition or movies.

252 MUSES. I have two people in mind when I design. The first is my usual client; the second is the one I want to conquer. I draw them; I put them on the notice board in the studio; I put names on both of them and get my team together to put together a profile of their habits: what each of them like to do, what they do when they go out at night, what kind of body they have, and what they like to show.

253 DEVELOPING A COLLECTION. To transfer the concept of the collection to each of the pieces, I choose details that symbolize the theme of each season. A recurring element in my collections is ruffles, and I have a different way of using them on each occasion that is in line with the chosen look.

254 MATERIALS. I have two groups of fabrics I work with in each collection. One of them is a fixture: silks, wools, and cashmeres varying in their weave depending on each season. The second group is changeable: they're the prints, brocades, and Jacquards. I choose them from the French, English, and Italian collections I look out for on my trips to Europe.

255 MANNEQUIN. My mannequin was custom made for me at a special workshop in Buenos Aires. We start with a size 8, then we move on to 10, 12, 14. Once the style is approved, we try the garment on a person to see it in movement. Sometimes I take the samples and I use them for a while to see how functional they are.

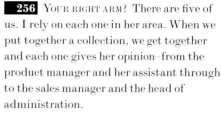

256 YOUR RIGHT ARM? There are five of us. I rely on each one in her area. When we put together a collection, we get together and each one gives her opinion–from the product manager and her assistant through to the sales manager and the head of administration.

257 STYLE. We work with high quality material, like natural silks in all varieties, and pure cottons. Crafting is evident in all of the details defining each garment: hand-rolling, embroidery, final seams. Exclusivity is linked to tradition. My clothes are designed to go with and enhance the personality of the wearer. This is what I consider to be the synthesis of elegance.

258 COMMUNICATION. Publicity is entrusted to a press agency, and I watch over every detail. For our big moment during the shows, we make sure of their diffusion in the most important media. We are very selective about whom we invite, about the press release we give, and the type of media.

259 CHALLENGE. We no longer just have to excel ourselves every six months now. Our demand means we now have to do mid-season collections. People get tired of seeing the same thing on a hanger all season and need something different all the time. This is why we make updates to each collection and we do a resort collection especially designed for summer in Punta del Este.

260 EVOLUTION. There is only one style; it doesn't change. It's my identity. I do try to keep with the times, to take up the challenge of being very up-to-date with everything going on in the arts, music, cinema, and theater. This gives me a much more current view of design and lifestyle. It helps me to not let my label age.

261 INSPIRATION. I experience each collection as a new chapter of one and the same story that unfolds with the changing seasons, and which I tell with varying degrees of awareness. The more I move forward, the more I take liberties with regard to a process that is schematic and linear. I learn to leave more room to chance—to chance encounters, to paradoxical associations, to clashes.

262 DEVELOPING A COLLECTION. I put a lot of thought into pieces that make up the collection by basing my ideas on the structure of the body, on anatomy. In my work with pleating, draping, and cutting, I interpret what should be soft or hard joints, curves, and folds. Collection after collection, you get to know yourself, to decipher your own creative identity. Things take shape naturally.

263 COLORS. I look for in-betweens, half-colors, soft colors, and ones that are difficult to put a name to. And I'm a white addict! The way I see it, color, or lack of color, is secondary to shape. I love that color can let you show off shape and material first; that the first thing your eyes notice is the construction.

264 TRADITIONAL MANUFACTURING VS. EXPERIMENTATION. I like to try out new things; I love cutting-edge styles and modernity, even after time has passed and left its mark. I love changing and romantic extravagance. I love things that question and disconcert; and I also like the incongruity they represent. Finally, and unfortunately, today's generations of know-how, crafts, and heritage have been marginalized.

265 BRAND VALUES. Buying a designer piece is a personal way of "consuming" fashion—an alternative back road compared to the fashion superhighway. However, I feel like a sponge soaking up the spirit of the times! So, what I offer is a choice that is both unique and rooted in our current collective existence.

266 COMMUNICATION STRATEGY. Buyers and clients are guests coming to discover a world of design. So you have to open the door to them; to give them the keys, so to speak. I try to create a connection, a kind of link between my world–my way of seeing things–and the sensitivity others feel. Relations with the press are at the heart of this strategy. Having a press office in Paris enables me to show my work to journalists.

267 STYLE. In my own modest ways, I try to design a daily choreography for the woman who wants to wear my clothes, a sort of poetic language.

268 PHILOSOPHY. For me, fashion design is a never-ending movement backwards and forwards between the range of intangible and fleeting feelings picked up on a street corner and the designer's individual sensitivity.

269 GOOD HABITS. What I find invaluable is to know yourself well. After that comes the task of identifying your own way of working.

270 SALES. A ready-to-wear collection sells well if the clothes are both unique and wearable. There is a huge amount of work to be done in order to sell what you make with regard to the kind of clientele, marketing, and publicity you have.

027

Eymèle Burgaud
www.eymele-burgaud.com

An initial education led her to a career in communications, first in Asia and then in France; several years later, she decided to rediscover her first passion: clothing and design. With diplomas from the fashion schools ESMOD (Paris) and the Lasalle International Fashion School (Singapore) in hand, and after a season working with John Galliano's studio, Eymèle Burgaud launched her first collection for S/S 05 presented during Paris Fashion Week. Graceful lines seem to belong to a world more fragile and poetic than our own. A compelling otherness leads us gently down roads less traveled. Her unabashedly feminine collections can be read as a reflection on the ideals of beauty and a re-reading of the 21st century female form. They are infused with a personal history rich in confrontations and unexpected yet rewarding turns.

© Valérie Belin

028 Gaspard Yurkievich
www.gaspardyurkievich.com

After his studies at Studio Berçot, Parisian Gaspard Yurkievich won the Festival d'Hyères in 1997 and launched his first prêt-à-porter women's collection in 1998. Since then, his shows have been an innovative launch pad that illustrate his sexy, contemporary, and urban visions. Gaspard has worked with such talents as the architect Didier Faustino, artist Edouard Leve, actress Elodie Bouchez, and musicians such as Matthew Herbert. Gaspard launched the men's prêt-à-porter and shoe collections in 2003. Keeping in line with his vision, the men's collection has since developed considerably and offers a wide range of dress shirts, T-shirts, and revisited masculine wardrobe classics. From 2005 to 2007, in parallel to his activity as fashion designer, he joined the teaching staff at the ENSAD arts school as a teacher of the fundamentals of fashion.

© Shoji Fujii

© Shoji Fujii

271 INSPIRATION. I find inspiration in fabrics and shapes, but I also react to what has been shown before. There's continuity in my design. It's more a way of moving, a step to be taken.

272 WORKPLACE. The studio and atelier are separate. The studio is where the designs are set down, and the atelier is where they are made up. It's very lively and messy. Journalists generally love it.

273 MATERIALS. There are pieces that respond very literally to the concept, and pieces that allow people to see what is behind. It's a matter of rhythm and taking a breath between pieces. I choose a fabric if I see the garment in my head when I touch it. I never say "never." It all depends on the design context; everything is beautiful when contextualized in an interesting way. I work with the same companies every season. These are the kind of "collaborators" involved in my work.

274 COLORS. An emotion. The way of working with the fiber gives it a brilliance or depth and this is the balance that completes my final choice.

275 TRADITIONAL MANUFACTURING VS. EXPERIMENTATION. I work around the Parisian couture heritage, with its tradition of thought and technique, but with a contemporary outlook.

© Shoji Fujii

© Alfredo Salazar   © Alfredo Salazar

276 YOUR RIGHT ARM? I have been working with Guido Voss, my partner, and with my brother, Damian Yurkievich, from the start.

277 COMMUNICATION. It's very important to build up a style with a very defined image. Runway shows are the means we have of getting our style across every season. We organize our publicity in-house.

278 PHILOSOPHY. I maintain the essence and the philosophy of the label with each season, with the make up and balance of the collections. But then I also have impulses with fabrics, shapes, with a trip, or with an artist.

279 IS FASHION ART? No, but there is a need to have an outlook for creating fashion that takes us close to the work of an artist. I often ask artists to participate in my shows to give them an emotional dimension that complements the collection.

280
SALES. I need to take into account the products that work in our company. Our network is small, making it easy to develop new ideas each season to cover the need for sales.

281 INSPIRATION. Experiment and have fun with what you're doing.

282 COLORS. Always wear black leather. It's sexy and black is flattering on any figure.

283 DEVELOPING A COLLECTION. Teach yourself new techniques, this way you get to put your own individual slant on it.

284 STYLE. Never follow color trends, work with palettes that you are comfortable with and that complement your vision. Stay away from neon...

285 EVOLUTION. Designing is all consuming and one can get lost in their own world. It's always good to find somebody to work with, even if you're doing completely different things! This will stop you from going crazy, and if it doesn't, at least you'll go crazy together.

286
PERSONALITY. Don't take yourself too seriously. Your supporters don't care about the little things that plague your mind.

287 YOUR RIGHT ARM? Networking is essential, especially when you are starting out as a young designer. Befriend photographers, stylists, make-up artists, etc. Within the industry people help each other especially at times of financial difficulty.

288 MISSION. This isn't an industry for the faint-hearted. It involves long hours with zero to minimal pay when starting out. You shouldn't go into fashion for money, you go into it for the passion of it all.

289 ADVICE. Never be satisfied, but always strive to be.

290 GOOD HABITS. Do good things and forget them, do bad things and remember them.

029 Gemma Slack
www.gemmaslack.com

The name Gemma Slack was featured among the names of emerging talents in London in 2009. This artist began her studies in fine arts at the Chelsea College of Art and Design, where she was encouraged to try fashion design. Enthusiastic about the idea of turning her paintings and sculptures into clothes, she enrolled in the Fashion Design Technology: Womenswear course at the London College of Fashion. After four years of work experience with Gareth Pugh, she presented her first, gothic-inspired collection for the S/S 09 season. Her unique flair for turning unusual materials into tailored pieces has captured the attention of a number of figures like the journalist Diane Pernet, the milliner Piers Atkinson, and the singer Róisín Murphy.

030

Georg Hieber
www.hieber.com.ar

This man has no need to draw attention with ridiculous outfits or hype. He conquers prudently—with materials, details, and finishing that set him apart from others. Georg Hieber advances in secret, with his German name, European touches, and Argentinean clients. This is a case in reverse—a European seeking Latin America. It is the story of a German who leaves behind a half-finished Berlin in order to construct a Buenos Aires. In his exclusive jewelry-store-like studio, located on Avenida Alvear in Buenos Aires, he likes to play hide-and-seek, with small windows and little on display. The mannequins are blindfolded and labels are subtly placed inside garments. The command to tone down is also obeyed in his designs, a concept he calls *neo-luxury,* because his styles feature elegance without the glitz.

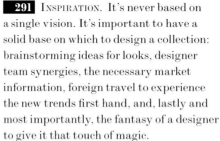

291 INSPIRATION. It's never based on a single vision. It's important to have a solid base on which to design a collection: brainstorming ideas for looks, designer team synergies, the necessary market information, foreign travel to experience the new trends first hand, and, lastly and most importantly, the fantasy of a designer to give it that touch of magic.

292 DEVELOPING A COLLECTION. For me, it was so important not only to have studied fashion design, but also patternmaking and dressmaking. This makes transferring an idea to paper easy, so each garment can be designed and made up. If the idea is clear and drawn up, it is very simple to follow the thread and adapt all of the designs to it. This is the essence of a designer, and it is where your performance can be seen.

293 COLORS. Strong colors always have a special place in my collections and are used for details and accessories as an intensifier. Most of the pieces are neutral colors; my basics are black, white, and natural tones.

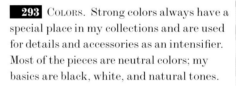

294 REFERENCES. I am restless by nature and need to be up-to-date at all times about what's happening in art, design, technology, and culture. Likewise, it is necessary to have the sensitivity to adapt yourself to what is happening in the world of politics, economics, and society.

295 TRADITIONAL MANUFACTURING VS. EXPERIMENTATION. The balance between tradition and experimentation is of extreme importance in fashion. Whatever the case, my label is based more on classical lines than cutting edge. The most important thing a firm has to achieve is a signature piece. In our case it's the raincoat, a perfect piece for any event or season.

296 COMMUNICATION. A brand doesn't exist without this, or at least it can't last. I personally handle all dealings with the press, media relations, and marketing. The message we have to put across is our DNA: femininity, elegance, and modernity. These are conveyed through a mixture of television, magazine, and newspaper appearances.

297 MATERIALS. The fabrics I choose are only made with natural fibers. In my opinion, the fabrics, the finishes, and any type of accessory have to be of the highest quality. I generally prefer fabrics with body, although there's nothing I definitively say "no" to. I'm currently adding linen and polyester to my collections, whereas I had never thought of using them before.

298 EVOLUTION. The concept of the label doesn't change with each season; but the collection always has to surprise and offer appealing novelties. Right now we are trying to create a younger and less formal look.

299 SALES. When putting together a collection, designers need to have a view to marketing the garments; they have to know what clients are looking for and adapt to their needs. A marketable collection has to be varied and offer a range of intelligent prices. It should also be wearable.

300
GOOD HABITS. Designers have to be hard-working, obsessive with their ideals, and perfectionists with details. They have to love what they do, be creative, and never grow tired of the ups and downs. Nothing is given to you in life; you have to fight and exert yourself to reach your goals, and it helps to have a little luck on your side.

301 INSPIRATION. Each collection revolves around the world of polo. The creative process begins with the many tournaments in different cities around the world, which inspire the season's collection. I think about the people taking part in the international polo circuit; not just about the players. Attention is also drawn to those following the sport: the people who, directly or indirectly, create a sophisticated, refined, and elegant image of this sport and the lifestyle attached to it.

302 WORKPLACE. My table is a constant source of ideas, either as pictures, infinite fabric swatches, inspirational garments, details of the sewing to keep in mind, the technical team, and specialist publications. Many notions come from there, which are later processed and applied to the finished product. Testing is carried out on people who collaborate in evaluating the garment through their feedback, either to remove possible flaws or to touch up specific details.

303 MATERIALS. Materials are always chosen for their quality. For example, we use French fabrics with characteristic designs for women's shirts, and Italian prints for the men's shirts that have become our trademark. We use noble and exclusive materials like mercerized Peruvian pima cotton for knitted garments, cashmere and Italian lambswool for sweaters, and special linens for pants and summer shirts.

304 TRADITIONAL MANUFACTURING VS. EXPERIMENTATION. The Argentinean polo tradition is the backbone of the La Martina style. Starting with this rich and vast source, all of the products that make up each collection are developed. La Martina is immediately recognized for its polo clothing inspired by historical matches and the highest level tournaments around the world.

305 BRAND VALUES. La Martina goes beyond the limits of clothing as part of an integrated collection of accessories, perfumes, and technical equipment specially-designed for players and their requirements. Consequently, we have a comprehensive and overall vision of the polo tradition, with a premium product that increases in value over time.

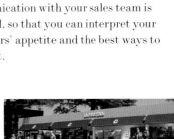

306 COMMUNICATION. Visual merchandising is extremely important. A special and inviting atmosphere is created through the structure of each sales space and the positioning of the product. Each sales outlet has its image worked on depending on its location. The Mediterranean spirit predominates in St. Tropez and Mykonos, with white fittings, blue walls, and light décor. However, the store on Avenida Alvear in Buenos Aires, which is specially-devoted to leather, has noble furnishings in polished wood, designer armchairs, and carpet.

307 EVOLUTION. La Martina possesses an individual style that hasn't changed with the passing of time. We have always made an effort to evolve, grow, and improve in all aspects through our strategy of introducing new raw materials and employing superior manufacturing. Collection after collection, we work very hard to develop and perfect the details. We contact international suppliers and travel in search of alternatives to the cutting edge market.

308 PHILOSOPHY. Fashion is an essential part of people's lives, whether or not they are aware of it. It's a daily choice we make to express our personality and place in the world. Today there are countless influences molding a trend, including somewhat unconventional places and situations compared to previous decades. There is no specific trend, just lots of different roads to take. The work of designers is to know their clients. They must select and interpret elements from this mass of influences and translate them into tangible objects that are adapted to clients' needs.

309 SALES. I don't believe there is an infallible formula for ensuring the commercial success of a collection. There is however a record of past successes that should be evaluated in great detail, which can help you to channel your career. Fluid communication with your sales team is essential, so that you can interpret your customers' appetite and the best ways to satisfy it.

310 GOOD HABITS. The most important is to be constantly informed and updated about the world surrounding us. It's very important to absorb information so that we can reach our own conclusions, which can later be tranferred to the product. Beyond any normal tendencies, you have to know how to become detached, and not to be afraid of going with a single concept. This is the only way you will be able to endure, leaving an imprint and creating a specific and unmistakable identity.

031

Geraldine Cunto/La Martina
www.lamartina.com

Buenos Aires, New York, and Florence are three wonderful, totally different cities brimming with culture, where anyone would want to spend at least some time. This is exactly what Geraldine Cunto has done. She studied in the Big

Apple and Tuscany before touching down in the Argentine capital where she works as a designer for La Martina. This exclusive clothes label is devoted to the world of polo, a sport where Argentina is an outstanding force, and creates pieces

for fans of the sport and those who live its lifestyle, as well as the players themselves. In fact, La Martina's design, quality, and prestige have led it to being recently named official supplier to the Federation of International Polo.

032

Gori de Palma
www.goridepalma.com

Gori de Palma's work revolves around black. His imagination is backed up by sound tracks. His style is imbued with post-punk, industrial, dense, strict, and sexual currents. For Gori de Palma, fashion has more than three dimensions–it is a space for action and a support for his different creative urges. It is as if each of this Majorcan's collections, advertising campaigns, and castings were reflections of his experiences and personal obsessions. The result of this exploration is a finely-honed, dark, and solid signature label with perverse undertones. Trained in fashion, patternmaking, fabric design, printing, and styling, Gori de Palma has collaborated with Swarovsky, Vans, and American Apparel, in addition to his work as a stylist on Andrés Calamaro's music videos and Volkswagen advertising campaigns.

311 INSPIRATION. I look for a specific theme for each collection. First I analyze the aesthetic values that transcend the particular theme. From then on, I try to create my own original and coherent universe.

312 COLORS. I look for shade and light in color. I mainly work with black, in all its hues. It's a real challenge to analyze the infinite possibilities this color has.

313 MATERIALS. I buy almost all my fabrics in Barcelona. The choice of fabric is determined by the quality, shade, price, and its technical qualities. Fabrics should be able to convey the concept of a collection, while being practical and long-lasting for the end customer. I avoid synthetics completely because, for me, cloth should be like a second skin—soft, delicate, and enduring.

314 WORKPLACE. My test dummy is a bare element I attack without any pre-meditated ideas. I like to experiment as I go, moving on and observing. There's no reason to limit yourself without moving forward, like in music. My table? Sixteen and a half feet long by seven feet wide. I start in the morning with an empty table; but by the end of the day, it's full of papers, rulers, ashtrays, coffees, magazines, and scissors.

315 COMMUNICATION. Thanks to publicity, you can turn your product into something more sensational. It's all about sharing your emotions and ideas with others. I don't handle it personally; although I would advise anyone starting out with a label to become associated with a press agency and to gradually place their trust in it. That's extremely important.

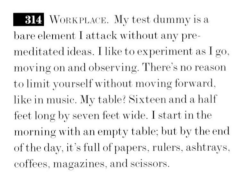

316 TRAINING. Speaking from where I am now, I can say that I learned my best lessons from two people. Ángel, for one, my design teacher, passed on values such as overcoming obstacles, innovation, and well-thought-out work. And then there's Óscar, my former art director, who helped me find my own language to express myself. He also gave me the guidelines for turning a garment into a dream.

317 STYLE. My label is a dream factory. I think people expect me to go where no one else has gone. For me, Gori de Palma is a synonym of freedom, tradition, breaking rules, and everything that is as far away as possible from the strictly conventional.

318 SALES. Although the market is increasingly unpredictable, there are basic factors, such as a commercial network, a good selection of international fairs and, in particular, a surprising, realistic, and impeccable collection. Even if your inspiration comes from inside, you should keep your eyes open to what's going on around you and be aware that fashion involves clothes to be used and lived in. It's not enough to be fashionable; you also have to be intelligent.

319 PHILOSOPHY. I don't believe in democratization or in exclusivity. I don't even believe in seasons. People travel and globalization is inevitable. Also, people are tired of being deceived and being told what is or isn't fashion. That's something that will mark our generation. They're showing major individuality.

GORI DE PALMA
spring - summer 2009

320
EVOLUTION. You're only as good as your next collection. The past is in the past; it was sold; it was shown; and it could always have been done better. That's why I'm always proud of my last collection; and of the one that's coming; of the one that takes the most out of me to put together; the one that forces me to excel myself; the one that excites me the most; and the one gives me a burst ulcer from nerves. Damn it!

321 INSPIRATION. I always think about movement of the shapes and sensation when I design and also the relationship between fluidity and structure, balanced constructions, and the rejection of accepted codes. It reflects the duality between fragility and strength coming together into a delicate but well-structured outline. Clothes are objects from a distance. When you wear them, they become space.

322 MANNEQUIN. I work on a Stockman mannequin customized by myself. I created this shape on a woman's body and ever since it has been my tool for working. I create my collections in my studio in the Marais neighborhood in Paris. I work in a glass-roof space for drawing and illustration and in a workshop for the draping, patternmaking, and sewing.

323 MATERIALS. I prefer natural fabrics such as silk, wool, cotton, linen, and paper fabric and leather that come from Italy, UK, Japan, and France. I try to never use synthetic fabrics that come from petroleum because I have a deep conscious about recycling. I overlap the most precious

materials. Fusing different materials together is a constant in my work. I combine leather and silk, leaving the rough edges visible.

324 TRADITIONAL MANUFACTURING VS. EXPERIMENTATION. I work on tradition and experimentation at the same time. I try to manage both of them. As for the representative item in my collection, I usually develop a special shape, be it a dress or a raincoat or accessories that carry the concept of the collection. I also work with kimonos. For me they are a symbol of history and exoticism, without buttons or closures, no locks, no keys.

325 INDIVIDUALITY VS. GROUP BELONGING. My work invokes mostly individuality but these people belong to a certain type of group within which there is an intimate connection that brings menswear and women's fashion closer through tailoring and draping–an interplay between masculine and feminine, expressing unseen sensuality and an unending harmonious duality.

326 COMMUNICATION. Yes, communication in the fashion business is very important and I have someone to help me take charge of it. We like to work with architecture, art, and design magazines. The fashion press we work with is very connected to the art worlds.

327 EVOLUTION. Yes, it is very important to renovate and renew every six months, but at the same time to keep a brand's signature silhouettes and colors. I normally work on a grey pallet, as a mix of all other colors. This neutral color is brightened and warmed by overlaying a rose carné, a plum violet, a green tea, and a nuance of taupe. The line of models is defined by the color black for a more precise graphic style.

328 IS FASHION ART? I create objects of art using clay, paper, and toile. It is a way to experiment and express my vision of form and space. I work with porcelain, which is a privileged material, and through it I can research the body to define the shape and to thus become the only constructive principle. Porcelain keeps the memory of fabrics, which I mix into the paste to create draped forms to mimic the natural sliding of fabric over the skin.

329 ADVICE. Best lesson I have learned is being vigorous and exigent with oneself.

330 SALES. What makes for good sales is working on techniques and trying to find out structure solutions. The commercial value of a brand is at the heart of good fashion development. Good sales give me confidence to move forward and keep on going.

033

Gustavo Lins
www.gustavolins.com

Brazilian Gustavo Lins was originally destined to be an architect. He actually graduated as one in his native country in 1989 before moving to Barcelona to study for his master's degree at the Polytechnic University of Catalonia. The following year, he began to work as a freelance patternmaker for such exclusive names as Jean-Charles de Castelbajac, Jean Paul Gaultier, Louis Vuitton, and John Galliano until 2003, when he created his own label, Gustavolins. His designs still continue to involve an architectural thought process. In fact, his logo is an inverted T-square, which says a lot about his ideology. It symbolizes balanced construction while rejecting accepted codes, and reflects the duality between fragility and strength that converge in the delicate but well-structured silhouettes he constructs.

034

Harry Halim
www.hhharryhalim.com

Indonesian-born and Singapore-based fashion bon vivant, Harry Halim is the quintessential designer's designer. He launched his first collection, BIAS, with startlingly delicately-draped pieces in black and red and was greeted with critical acclaim and overwhelming press response in 2006. He was crowned winner at the Asian Young Fashion designer contest with this collection. He was also announced finalist at the Mercedes-Benz Asia Fashion Awards in the same year. Supremely sensual, quietly romantic, and decisively precise with an underlying tone of danger describes the aesthetic of the very individual Harry Halim woman. Inspired by fragile emotions, the sensitivity given in each garment is a mix of volume and asymmetry. Recently Harry contributed to the Singapore Design Festival where he collaborated and curated an exhibition called "Moonlies."

331 INSPIRATION. Every collection for me begins with my mood, my emotions, and the environment that surrounds me at that time. It doesn't have to start with a theme. Themes can always be created and fixed after the collection is done.

332 MANNEQUIN. They are full of thin ribbons and pins in the messy studio.

333 MATERIALS. Working on tailoring materials and luxurious fabrications and leather is my favorite because they will give a good effect after you put them on your body. I am not a big fan of linen even though it is comfortable for summer.

334 STYLE. I wanted to showcase the flip side of a coin and how beauty can be derived from different things.

335
TRADITIONAL MANUFACTURING VS. EXPERIMENTATION. Balancing the traditional and the modern together, so the outcome will be neither too traditional nor too modern.

336 EVOLUTION. Oh for sure! I need to. In fact not every six months but everyday!

337 CHALLENGE. I just can't get out from the dark side of every collection. Creating a fun, relaxed, and happy collection is just not my thing.

338 STREET FASHION VS. FASHION DESIGNER. Fashion comes from the creativities and the great ideas of designers, from the early stage of development to the final outcome.

339 GOOD HABITS. It's about your own taste.

340 SALES. Something that's easy to wear and of a dark color is always a good sales item. Sometimes, as long as we understand the targeting customer, it is easy to go on to each step.

342 INSPIRATION. An idea for me is paramount. I always imagine the heroine of my collections. Anastasia, Lolita, Anna Karenina, a girl-warrior–all of them are visible for me. I try to create her character with the help of design language and design instruments.

343 MATERIALS. We use only natural materials, not synthetic. Twice a year we choose fabrics during the Première Vision exhibition in Paris. I like classical materials, like silk and wool, to more cutting-edge, like fur-like cotton.

344 YOUR RIGHT ARM? A team of my assistants. All of them! They help me to do that huge volume of design.

345 BRAND VALUES. Individuality of our clothing and its excellent quality are two things which stand out for our brand and are appreciated most by the Chapurin customer. "Deluxe" for us is in the first line–the value of the uncompromised quality rather than price.

341 MANNEQUIN. Actually we have no definite preferences towards models, in terms of nationality, human type, etc. The professionalism of a model is most important for us. the choice of model also depends on the style of a collection and its idea.

346 COMMUNICATION. We create individuality. We give people the opportunity to look better. We are a luxury brand, so all statements we do, all shootings we organize, all interviews we give, we do only with professionals and with authoritative media. The main media activity of our brand is concentrated in the PR field. We support very good relationships with top magazines, newspapers, and TV channels by making events and keeping personal relations with journalists.

347 IS FASHION ART? Sometimes I do art. I hope so. But I don't think that fashion is an art. Only in our haute couture collections are we approaching the idea of art.

348 STREET FASHION VS. FASHION DESIGNER. The general essence of fashion is a mix of ideas. Streets take them from media, media from designers, and designers are inspired by street fashion.

349 GOOD HABITS. You should be a perfectionist, a good time-manager, and you should learn to catch and remember all bright impressions and to pay great attention to details.

350 ACKNOWLEDGEMENT. I appreciate the praise of fashion professionals, like fashion editors such as Aliona Doletskaya (Russian *Vogue*) and leading fashion critics like Suzy Menkes–my best clients.

035

Igor Chapurin
www.chapurin.com

A veteran of Russian fashion design, Igor Chapurin started his career at a very early age. For three generations, the Chapurins have been innovating and reinventing fashion in Russia. His grandfather was a pioneer in the Russian linen manufacturing business, his father successfully managed many sewing enterprises, and his mother directed a headwear factory. Igor's first important step was in 1993 when he created the dresses for the Miss Europe, Miss World, and Miss Universe pageants. In 1995 Chapurin showed his first collection, "To Russia with Love," in the Red Hall of Metropol Hotel in Moscow. His flaring style charmed many and, always looking for new challenges, Igor went on to collaborate with theater companies, and opened his line of jewelry, furniture, and home accessories.

© Alex Fadel

036

Imane Ayissi
www.imaneayissi.com

Hailing from Cameroun, the son of a family of artists and sportsmen: his father was a champion boxer, his mother had been elected Miss Cameroun in 1960, and his brothers and sisters are dancers and singers. He worked as a model, presenting men's collections and brands such as Cardin, Dior, Lanvin, Givenchy, Yves Saint Laurent, and Valentino. The garments of Imane Ayissi's couture and prêt-à-porter lines meld African traditions with western fashion. His collections, often featuring exotic, evocative names, combine craftsmanship, materials, and traditional African cuts. Together with his use of innovative fabrics there is also often an infusion of typically African-style DIY or recycling work, references to Parisian haute couture, and contemporary creativity to create a fashion targeted at an international public.

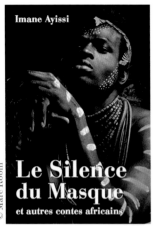

Imane Ayissi

Le Silence du Masque

et autres contes africains

© Marc Robin

© Raffaele Soccio and Luca Sorrentino for Alta Roma

351
TRADITIONAL MANUFACTURING VS. EXPERIMENTATION. In my opinion, the definition of fashion is experimentation and innovation, so I always try to create something new, even surprising at times. But innovation should also be based on tradition, whether a little bit or a lot. Thinking of creating something from nothing is an illusion. In the high-fashion range, a collection is a very accurate exercise: for each collection you have to create garments representative of your style, garments representatives of the collection theme, spectacular outfits for press, more simple and affordable outfits for clients...and all these items must be very coherent.

352 INSPIRATION. Everything can inspire me to start a collection: object, picture, materials, words, story, construction principle, smell, etc. Then I put words on this inspiration and it becomes the real theme of the collection. For example, my summer 2007 collection "Le Printemps de Satan" came from my desire of mixing gothic with romantic. All the challenge is then translating this theme in outlines, garments, details, and more in an intelligent way.

353 MATERIALS. Actually I can use every kind of fabric, but because I am more interested in the construction and the architecture of the garments, I use more plain fabrics. I choose them for their qualities (fluidity, density, weight, softness, etc.) which must correspond to the outlines of the final garment I want. I can even use very basic fabrics, like cotton jersey, and "re-build" them into a sophisticated material. For example, for my 09/10 winter collection "Voodoo Mood," I created dresses made entirely out of tied ribbons, cut in a very simple bamboo jersey. I am more and more involved in earth protection, so I look more and more for organic fabrics, but it's still very hard to find organic fabrics that are a little bit sophisticated.

354 YOUR RIGHT ARM? My business partner and friend Jean-Marc Chauve, who is also designer, art advisor, and consultant at the Institut Français de la Mode (IFM), the prestigious French fashion school and research center.

355 INDIVIDUALITY VS. GROUP BELONGING. I didn't study in any fashion school and while I come from a continent (Africa) with clothes, jewelry, and other finery traditions, it lacks a fashion tradition. Fashion is a western invention and so I had to choose my influences and references by myself. Therefore I think I'm more on the individual side, and maybe my best creations are interesting because it's hard to characterize them (Is it African? European? Haute couture? Avant-garde?) But of course, as every designer, I'm influenced by several creative works, from several creative areas: fashion design, architecture, plastic arts, music.

© Alex Fadel

© Raffaele Soccio and Luca Sorrentino for Alta Roma

356 CHALLENGE. As a designer, I need to improve myself, to search and to innovate all the time. Every six months is still the basic fashion rhythm, it may even be faster now with cruise, resort, and pre-collections. It doesn't always correspond to my own rhythm; sometimes it's too long and you can become tired of an idea or a collection. Other times, it's too short when you want to explore a deeper idea or theme. You have to adapt to this structure, constraints are necessary to creation.

357 IS FASHION ART? I used to be a dancer of African and contemporary dance, but now I write. I have written two books of tales in French mixed with my African native language, the Ewondo language, *Millang Mi Ngorè-Histoires du Soir* and *Le Silence du Masque*. A lot of fashion designers are also photographers, graphic designers, plastic artists–all are visual arts like fashion. I'm more of a designer-writer, and it may be that with my fashion collections I also try to tell stories.

358 STREET FASHION VS. FASHION DESIGNER. Today: both. Fashion travels between the street and the catwalk. Street creativity today, especially from teenagers, is a great inspiration to every designer, even those in luxury brands. At the same time, there are still very strong proposals from designers that are recycled by the street. For me it's great pleasure to imagine one of my designs being seen on the street. That's why I'm always open to collaborate with mass-market brands so as to produce cheaper garments, like the work I did for summer 2006 with La Redoute.

359 TRAINING. When I started to work as a fashion designer in Cameroon, I used to work in very bad conditions: no money, no structure, old machines, no choice for fabrics. It didn't prevent me from going on. You can always create, imagine, and innovate from almost nothing. So talent and creativity doesn't depend on your environment, or your money.

360 ADVICE. Be curious about everything!

© Stéphane de Bourgies

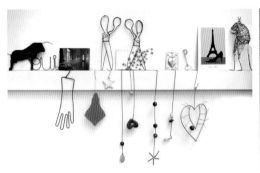

361 WORKPLACE. Our table is a little messy; it's full of things that inspire us, objects we like, and things we find in the street. We tend to try garments out on a model to see the effect of movement on them.

362 INSPIRATION. When we begin a collection, we think of the issues that worry and affect us at the time. We also have in mind the latest books we have read and exhibitions we have been to see, as well as the illustrators and painters we like. All of this influences us, and we use it by including it in an inspiration scrap book that helps us to work out prints and colors.

363 TRADITIONAL MANUFACTURING VS. EXPERIMENTATION. We love craft sewing techniques, hand work, embroidery, appliqué, ribbons, and buttons. We also like to experiment with prints. When we put together a collection, we don't think about doing a signature piece; but that

— doesn't mean we never want one to stand out. It's the public that chooses it as representative.

364 BRAND VALUES. We make special clothes and we put our heart in it. We feel that pieces have to last forever and never go out of fashion. That's why we don't follow trends much, and why we do what we feel like at all times. Everything about this society moves very fast and there is insatiable consumption. We never stop buying and throwing away. We want to make clothes that last for years.

365 MATERIALS. We choose natural fabrics becasue they are nicer on the skin. Clothes shouldn't only be beautiful; they should also be practical and comfortable. Lately, we have been including a lot of organic cotton in our collections because we are concerned about the devastating consequences of cotton farming.

366 EVOLUTION. We don't feel a lot of pressure from one season to the next. We try to do things the best we can; and this is the base we work on. We used to do runway shows, and the press reviews would impose on our work; but now that we are more focused on stores and clients we sell more than ever. We've also matured and place a higher value on happiness and tranquillity.

367 IS FASHION ART? Picasso made art. There are very few artist-designers, maybe three or four. Everyone else is a designer who wants to produce art... and the outcome is awful, don't you think?

368 SALES. The best reward for our label is to see that our clothes don't age and that people keep using and loving them.

369 COMMUNICATION. We have a publicity agency that makes very good choices about our appearance in the media. We also communicate directly with our clients through our blog and Facebook. We love Internet tools for explaining our philosophy. And we also receive feedback.

370
ADVICE. It's all about making clothes people will want to wear. Sometimes, when you're studying or are just beginning, you think about yourself, about your references, and the things you like. You forget what others might like. We've learned to make what we like, but we haven't stopped making things other people will understand and will want to have.

037

Inés Aguilar, Iván Martínez/La Casita de Wendy
www.lacasitadewendy.com

Björk modeled these designers' creations on the front covers of *Vogue* and *Les Inrockuptibles*. That music should be such a strong influence is no coincidence. It comes from the passion architect Inés Aguilar and philosopher Iván Martínez—the partners behind La Casita de Wendy—and their feel for music. Since starting out in the world of fashion seven years ago, today they have outlets in New York, Tokyo, Hong Kong, Reykjavik, Paris, Madrid, and Barcelona, and present their collections at Berlin's Bread & Butter and Paris's Rendez-Vous fairs. Their creations feature a carefully chosen range of colors, simple shapes, and contrasting prints, not only in their own collections, but also in their collaborations with brand names in different fields, including rock bands and Absolut Vodka, and their advertising campaigns.

038

Iris van Herpen
www.irisvanherpen.com

This young designer hailing from Wamel, the Netherlands, represents an avant-garde couture image with a slight futuristic undertone. By experimenting with unusual materials and forms as well as searching for extremes, Iris van Herpen creates a new, unlimited world that tickles spectators, leaving an open horizon to their own interpretations. Iris van Herpen shows another vision of what is beautiful. Not everyone will have similar ideas seeing her creations and this is exactly what she strives for. After internships at Alexander McQueen and Claudy Jongstra, Iris van Herpen graduated at the ArtEZ Academy of Arts in Arnhem. Her graduation collection, as well as collections presented at two consecutive shows at the Amsterdam International Fashion Week (2007/08), were enthusiastically received by the national and international press.

371 INSPIRATION. I start looking for interesting materials and, when I find them, I experiment and try out different techniques and ways of working with them. Then I start thinking of the concept, not before, because I want to give myself the space and freedom of experiment in the beginning of my process.

372 WORKPLACE. It must be big enough to have a few dummies standing next to each other: you can look to them from a few meters distance so that you have an overview of your collection. Otherwise, you can loose the connection between the sets and overdo/overuse a material.

373 DEVELOPING A COLLECTION. I try not to focus too much on a concept, because it becomes too obvious very quickly. I only work with the atmosphere of my concept in the back of my head. Whatever style you have, never stick to the first ideas you get with a concept. I use a lot of leather because every piece is unique and different to work on. It has more power and personality than a fabric—and it is everlasting and timeless. In the end, it is not about what material you use but how you use it. If you are a good designer you can make something beautiful out of every fabric. But of course, the better the quality of a fabric or material, the better the outcome.

374 INDIVIDUALITY VS. GROUP BELONGING. I only make one offs. Fashion should be an expression of who you are. It is terrible for me to see so many people wearing the same clothes and looking the same without a personal style.

375
COMMUNICATION. It is easy in communication to lose your personality and present yourself as someone other than who you are. By doing that, you will find your brand as an actor and you will not be happy. From the beginning, try to show who you really are. That is one of the most difficult parts: to not pretend too much.

376 EVOLUTION. I think every collection is imperfect on some points. It can be done better the next time. I learn a lot with each collection, so I take that with me to the following one, therefore you try to get better and better.

377 STYLE. I retain experiment, avant-gardism, and futurism style and I change materials, shapes, and intension.

378 PHILOSOPHY. Fashion has different lives, but the art side of fashion is to individualize, as it is the expression of the designer and also the choice of the people of that time.

379 GOOD HABITS. Persistence, personality, and an unmistakable signature.

380 ADVICE. Learn from the people you admire for their work. Share thoughts, inspiration, and creativity with other professionals.

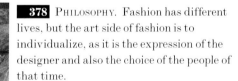
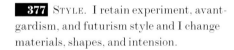
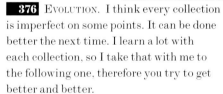

381 INSPIRATION. The method is always the same, and it is divided into two parts: First we brainstorm to reunite all those subjects and sensations that are going around in our head and are present in our lives at a certain moment. We always create from a present situation. Of these ideas, we select the most interesting ones to work together. From there, we begin to create abstract concepts and create new concepts from a mixture of these ideas. We form them in color, form, and fabric that is coherent to these new concepts.

382 DEVELOPING A COLLECTION. We create from the base, we don't transform nor do we adapt the pattern or forms, but each collection is an altogether new one. Each collection is dealt with in a different way and formed from complex concepts. We synthesize the idea and create new forms and silhouettes that project this idea. We go from the general to the individual, creating coherence throughout the collection. Each article of the collection has a sense and a meaning within the overall nature.

383 MATERIALS. We create the fabric that we need, then we choose the proportion of the components and the quality of those. We also dye the fabric to the exact color that we need until it's perfect. We make a selection of colors during the creative process that are of precisely thought-out tones and intensity. We are always investigating new technologies and new materials.

384 BRAND VALUES. Our aim in the future is to create our own universe, our own language, to have our own times, and to express our ideas in different forms, not only on the catwalk but with the aid of new platforms like the Internet, videoart, artistic installations, performances, and photography.

385 TRADITIONAL MANUFACTURING VS. EXPERIMENTATION. We live in a changing world that is constantly evolving, which causes a need for experimentation. We prefer the experimentation and the investigation in new forms, fabrics, concepts, and ways of communication. However, we cannot forget tradition. It is the base to continue growing.

386 COMMUNICATION. The communication is very important in Isaacymanu. It helps us to transmit the concept that we work with in each collection. It is very creative work, and our objective is that people receive the message that we want to express. We deal with communication and do iVideos, photos, web, etc. Our intention is that people who wear Isaacymanu feel identified with the images and the universe that we have created around the collection.

387 EVOLUTION. Our style comes from a mixture between what we have lived and what we are living. Every season something changes and something prevails, but Isaacymanu symbolizes ideas and images that are always present and clarify each collection. In each new collection we assume new challenges and we create new objectives. We feel the necessity to make new things, to experiment, and to learn, projecting our work at a higher level each time.

388 IS FASHION ART? Yes, each collection is like artwork. We do fashion, but we also do art, although we separate one thing from the other. What we do is the result of a translation of a complex idea to an article, and the artistic work is the context in which that idea has sense. We work the two disciplines with the same concept in each collection, and we then usually exhibit meetings in the same space, or concept-store.

389 GOOD HABITS. A designer is an observer, investigator, and creator. He analyzes the society, the mechanisms of the world in which he lives, and he tries to give an answer that he has observed. But the important thing is the daily work. A designer must investigate and experiment, reach conclusions and then break them, in order to always have a projection of the future and a vision of the present.

390 SALES. Stores in which we sell are spaces in agreement with our thoughts so that they interlace art and fashion. Those stores are designed to receive new ideas and to show artistic projects. Usually we accompany the collection of a creative shop window designed for that collection, and it's a creative stimulus for us to design each of these shop windows.

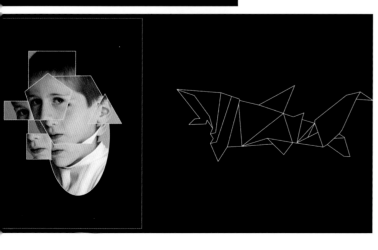

ISAACYMANU

039

Isaac Fabregat, Manuel Olarte/Isaacymanu
www.isaacymanu.com

As the hot new Spanish fashion design duo to come out in recent years, Isaacymanu have quickly been noticed and started to set trends. Isaac Fabregat and Manuel Olarte impress with geometry and science-formula-inspired designs, bright neon colors all condensed on oversize T-shirts and slim fit sweaters and fleece. They cite disco culture, ice, and the bottom of the sea as inspirations and the result couldn't be any quirkier. After meeting in Madrid in 2003, they decided to relocate to fashion hotspot Paris some years later, only to mention London as their next hub. Clearly, postmodern city-hopping is another of their influencing drives. Their F/W 09 collection, "Sous le Prisme," is inspired by light effects as they pass through a prism, and it has received a wealth of press coverage and retail success.

040

Isabela Capeto
www.isabelacapeto.com.br

After learning the trade at the Accademia di Moda in Florence, Italy almost 15 years ago, Isabela Capeto has become a shining light in the firmament of Brazilian fashion design. Before creating her own designer label, Isabela spent some time in creative environments of important designers such as Maria Bonita, Maria Bonita Extra, and Lenny, as well as having worked with prints in the Bangu factory. In April 2003, she finally inaugurated her own atelier in Rio de Janeiro. Isabela possesses a unique method of creating her collections. She is inspired by museums and books, never by predetermined trends. Each piece is like a work of art: handmade, always embroidered, dyed, or plissé, with many attachments of old lace, sequins, tulle, or fabric trims. Her object is always–in her own words–"to make women feel beautiful wearing romantic clothes."

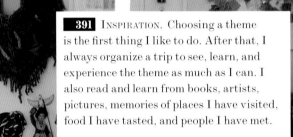

391 INSPIRATION. Choosing a theme is the first thing I like to do. After that, I always organize a trip to see, learn, and experience the theme as much as I can. I also read and learn from books, artists, pictures, memories of places I have visited, food I have tasted, and people I have met.

392 WORKPLACE. It is located in an antique house, on a calm street in Rio de Janeiro surrounded by trees and birds in a very quiet neighborhood. The decoration is very colorful, which inspires my imagination. My office has a big white table in the center and many drawings, books, posters, and pictures all around.

393 COLORS. I love colorful clothes. I think colors lift you up and make people look happy and in a good mood. I work with a color pale in each collection and I love when I can make it as colorful as possible.

394 YOUR RIGHT ARM? My right arm is Eduarda Braga, a really good friend and an amazing professional!

395 BRAND VALUES. My collections evoke individuality, each piece has a lot of personality and anyone who dresses in Isabela Capeto will be well-dressed, with a unique style.

396
MISSION. I am inspired by museums and books, never by predetermined trends. Each piece is like a work of art: handmade, always embroidered, dyed or plissé, with many attachments of old lace, sequins, tulle, or fabric trims. My main objective is to make women feel beautiful wearing romantic clothes.

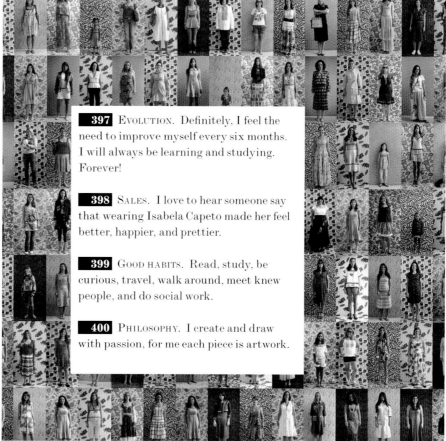

397 EVOLUTION. Definitely, I feel the need to improve myself every six months. I will always be learning and studying. Forever!

398 SALES. I love to hear someone say that wearing Isabela Capeto made her feel better, happier, and prettier.

399 GOOD HABITS. Read, study, be curious, travel, walk around, meet knew people, and do social work.

400 PHILOSOPHY. I create and draw with passion, for me each piece is artwork.

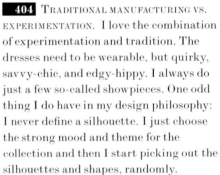

401 INSPIRATION. I always work that way. I do a kind of script, as if I were creating a story within a strong, feeling-based fairytale and mood world. Then, I just start choosing things there–adding colors, shapes, textures…kind of filling up the frame.

402 WORKPLACE. I live in a loft in Williamsburg, Brooklyn. I work at home. Huge windows, lots of daylight, trains passing by, with the Williamsburg bridge in front of me. I have one big, white table with everything on it that I do need, including two computers–sometimes I'm so restless, that I can't wait for a file to download and I need to use two Macs working at the same time.

403 MATERIALS. I use a few southern European material manufacturers and my jerseys come from Finland. The materials need to have strong character. I never look at the price. Our collection is so wild-minded and artsy that I don't think of the commercial side at all. All of our dresses are very wearable. It's my philosophy to do "pieces of wearable art."

404 TRADITIONAL MANUFACTURING VS. EXPERIMENTATION. I love the combination of experimentation and tradition. The dresses need to be wearable, but quirky, savvy-chic, and edgy-hippy. I always do just a few so-called showpieces. One odd thing I do have in my design philosophy: I never define a silhouette. I just choose the strong mood and theme for the collection and then I start picking out the silhouettes and shapes, randomly.

405 INDIVIDUALITY VS. GROUP BELONGING. Both, always. They are really off-mainstream pieces, but everyone that wears one and meets someone else wearing one feels like they are still one-of-a-kind but also soulmates. I personally feel even closer to anyone I see on the street wearing my dresses. It's a little IVANAhelsinki tribe, where cool chicks share a rocker-girl attitude with hippy-twisted, bohemian-glamour style.

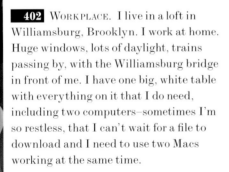
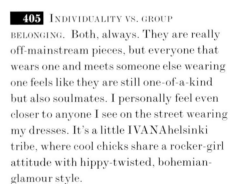

406
COMMUNICATION STRATEGY. We don't have any strategy. I have to say that there are so many manmade structures and rules in the world, that I always enjoy something that still has free flow, spontaneous moves, madness with respect and reasonability, passion, and hardwork. That's our strategy.

407 STYLE. It retains the feeling of vagabond chicks and a certain aesthetic of the rocker type of hippy girl that's on the road and living the dream. It's a bit romantic, savvy, and bohemian, with Scandinavian moods and Slavic flavor. Sometimes it gets romantic (antique and darker), sometimes more Scandinavian (light and graphic). Those are the worlds that it keeps mixing and matching always.

408 STREET FASHION VS. FASHION DESIGNER. I think fashion nowadays has gone to too much engineering work. It's too structured and commercially driven rather than having come from the streets, from charismatic, endearing individuals, that live strongly. Fashion picks up their moods and sells these free-soul dreams to the ones not daring enough to live them.

409 ADVICE. Be truthful to yourself. Never do anything that you don't believe in.

410 SALES. I've decided to outsource myself from thinking about the money. My sister and I have decided to work that way. We only need enough money to keep the business running with no assistance from outside investors. That guarantees us the free playground to do the things we love.

© Knotan

041

Ivana Helsinki
www.ivanahelsinki.com

Paola Ivana Suhonen is the artist behind the label IVANAhelsinki and designs all of its pieces that are born from northern legends, western romances, and her own dark and naïf mental landscapes. Besides designing clothes, she designs the prints and graphics associated with the label, always with the support of her sister, Pirjo. Each IVANAhelsinki garment is made in Finnish factories, with a manufacturing philosophy based on ethics and respect for the environment that also keeps to the methods and details of typical Finnish craftsmanship. This way of focusing her designs has led her to make a name for herself over ten years in current fashion circles and to be the only Scandinavian women's label to show during Paris Fashion Week.

042

Jane McMillan/Mac Millan
www.mac-millan.com

The company was founded in 1997 by its designer Jane McMillan to carve a niche in the fashion universe with her unique vision of color and texture. Jane was born in the small sea-side town of Stranraer which has been a major source of inspiration for her print designs. She moved to London to study womenswear at the London College of Fashion where she won many awards for design including one from the British Council presented by Lady Diana. She has been a visiting lecturer at Central Saint Martins College and, rather than work at international fashion house Jill Sander, launched her first collection stocked by the London boutique Koh Samui. Jane is a consultant for the governments sector advisory board for design and in 2007 was nominated for Scottish Designer of the Year.

411 INSPIRATION. Using a theme helps to focus my ideas. It also makes it easier for public relations to promote collections to the press.

412 WORKPLACE. My studio was designed to make maximum use of space and light, with skylight windows, a large cutting table, sewing table, and mannequin for draping. Cupboards are filled to the brim with brightly colored trimmings, threads, and rolls of fabric, and on the wall there is an enormous mood board with sketches of the current collection. I keep referring to this throughout the design and sampling process in order to remain true to the collection theme.

413 COLORS. Color is very important for my designs and is one of the most fundamental elements in projecting the mood of a collection.

414 TRADITIONAL MANUFACTURING VS. EXPERIMENTATION. It is important to experiment with new techniques, however new developments should only be a fairly small percentage of the collection. It is essential to retain signature styles that have already proven themselves in the market.

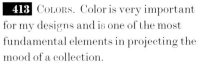

415 BRAND VALUES. The Mac Millan brand name is inspirational, stylish, luxurious, and colorful.

416 COMMUNICATION. Good communication is important to all areas of the business, whether it is conveying the new collection to press and buyers, explaining ideas to the studio team, or communicating with other creatives as well as factories.

417 STREET FASHION VS. FASHION DESIGNER. Fashion is a melting pot of ideas between the street and the designers. Sometimes the street is influenced by designers and at times designers are influenced by the street.

418 ACKNOWLEDGEMENT. The best praise I have ever received for my work was to be nominated for Scottish Designer of the year. This was particularly significant since the judges included the highly respected Kate Phelan, fashion director of British *Vogue*, and Hilary Alexander of *The Daily Telegraph*.

419 STYLE. The styles evolve each season retaining Mac Millan's signature look of femininity, colorful prints, and quality. Details and shapes change depending on the desired look for each collection.

420 ADVICE. John Galliano's first backer said: "There are three ways to succeed in this industry: 1. work, 2. hard work, and 3. harder work."

18 front

layers of silk chiffon all caught together at underbust seam

bodice is mounted on habotai, then pleated and bagged out at top edge with 3rd layer of lining.

underskirt is crepe de chine joined to habotai below hip level. Habotai is then attached at underbust seam along with tiers of chiffon

this is then lined with habotai.

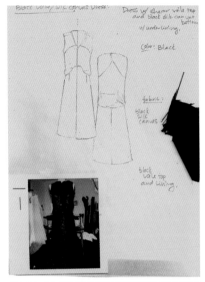

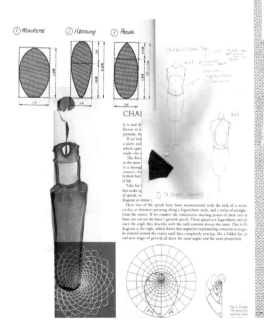

421 INSPIRATION. I sometimes think about themes and sensations, but often only as a starting point to develop a narrative. I am most inspired by creating a story. In addition to a narrative, I imagine the woman, the context, the moment in the interior or exterior space she will be in when she is wearing the finished garment.

422 WORKPLACE. I am fortunate to work in a beautiful space that was formerly a ballet studio. It has hardwood floors and floor-to-ceiling windows. The floors still have the marks of the dancers. It's filled sparingly with antique furniture that I have found, along with objects and images that I feel represent me. It is a hidden gem in Los Angeles and really reflects my aesthetic.

423 MATERIALS. Fabric comes with its own associations and personality. I like to use certain fabrics that already carry associations and reinvent those associations. I like fabrics that will translate the shapes that I am thinking about and/or will give me the ability to sculpt with them. I would probably refrain from using fur, a pre-existing print, or stretch lace.

424 TRADITIONAL MANUFACTURING VS. EXPERIMENTATION. I enjoy both tradition and experimentation; they are equally important in my work–to take something classic and use it as a constraint. It's very important to develop representative items in each collection, and it is crucial for branding. The fun lies in figuring out what those items are over time.

425 COMMUNICATION STRATEGY. We are not trendy. We are designing for a woman who likes to play with the notion of classic. We design for a woman who is willing to take a risk. Our imagery and press materials reflect this aesthetic and we work with artists and photographers who possess a similar outlook.

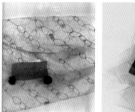

426
BRAND VALUES. Although surprisingly my collections may be "on trend" in different ways, it is not something that is important to me. I believe our creations invoke and celebrate individuality, and I see this in the women who buy my clothes. They are more interested in unique, detailed pieces or artisanal clothing evocative of style or intellectual ideas, rather than "fashion."

427 STYLE. My style always retains sculptural elements, clean lines, and organic shapes. It goes in and out in its femininity, sometimes reflecting a more androgynous tomboy spirit.

428 STREET FASHION VS. FASHION DESIGNER. I believe it's both. It is important to look at all of it. We see that new ideas both trickle up and down. They are different reactions or interpretations to the same world.

429 GOOD HABITS. It's different for everyone. For me, organization is the key and allows me to think more freely. Managing deadlines and your calendar are crucial. Working on these two things will always save you time, money, and stress. Its great to use last-minute time to push yourself creatively and fine-tune what you have developed.

430 SALES. Sales are obviously important and have to be thought about somewhat during development. This is true whether you have your own business or are designing for someone else's brand. I believe the best thing for sales is clarity of vision and strong design. Develop your brand in the process so that buyers want to buy into the brand, long term.

043

Jasmin Shokrian
www.jasminshokrian.com

From an early age, Jasmin Shokrian has been immersed in the pleasures of handcrafted clothing and in the gratification inherent in the philosophy of fashion as art. Born and raised in Los Angeles, she counts her mother, who was taught how to sew in an Iranian finishing school, as her first and primary influence. Living in various countries as a child, Shokrian eventually channeled the gift of her artistic and culturally rich upbringing into a career in various creative medias. She opted instead for the Art Institute of Chicago, graduating with a BFA in film, painting, and sculpture. Soon after, Shokrian founded a collective with several other Chicago artists, exploring three-dimensional sculpture, often using fabric as a medium. Eventually these projects organically evolved into the production of clothing and other wearable objects.

044

Jessica Trosman
www.trosman.com

Although Jessica Trosman is making more of a name for herself in the fashion world through her trosman label, she refuses to leave Buenos Aires, the city where she finds her inspiration. She is also a great admirer of *National Geographic* magazine and feels nostalgia for legendary, ground-breaking architects like Charles Eames, Frank Lloyd Wright, Le Corbusier, and Mies van der Rohe, which motivates her to design garments using different methods than other fashion designers. She decides on a silhouette by making scientific decisions and creates each piece as if it were an architectural project, making each part appear assembled instead of sewn. These delightful constructions are currently on sale in prestigious stores in Europe, Asia, and the US.

431

INSPIRATION. We work continuously and constantly; we never "start" a collection. When there is a commercial need or a communicative need to present a collection, we show a selection of our latest designs at that time.

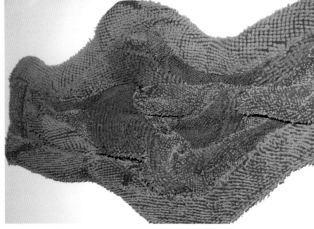

432 DEVELOPING A COLLECTION. We don't believe in the precision of design at all. The perfect drawing or computer-assisted design doesn't interest us. On the contrary, we like to think up and create solutions in a chaotic, circumstantial, and spontaneous way. The instruments of precision have no pride of place in our lives. It's much more important to become visually infected; to have a heap of ideas and not to find where we left our favorite.

433 MATERIALS. The choice of a material can be due to many things: by chance, triggered by a memory. We almost never like synthetics.

434 COLORS. We don't always look for the same thing in our choice of color. Sometimes we try to give a feeling of security; other times we try to confuse and irritate. It's like composing music and thinking about how the chords are used.

435 TRADITIONAL MANUFACTURING VS. EXPERIMENTATION. It isn't good to suggest that one should work in such a structured way. I never decided to have a signature piece, although some people say that we do. Afterwards it's good to become aware that such a thing exists, but only afterwards. The moment of creation should be chaotic and visceral.

436 BRAND VALUES. At the moment, the only thing my label promises and achieves is to satisfy my taste. The only thing I believe I'm capable of doing is what I find appealing. It just so happens that nobody is totally unique in their preferences, which is why there are people who seem to understand me. In any case, it's something I have no control over.

437 COMMUNICATION. Communication is something I have fun with. I don't know whether it's important or not, only that it's a part of the job that I really feel good about. I don't have any defined message or strategy to begin with. I don't see it as something separate from the design of products. I would never delegate it to anyone else because I see it as an integral part of what I'm offering. I don't think that first you have to design an object and then you have to design its communication. I believe the objects are integral parts of communication.

438 EVOLUTION. I don't believe in enhancement because I don't think it's intelligent to think of things as better or worse. Everything I do comes from that moment. I like to see what I do only as a testament to how I experienced that moment.

439 ADVICE. You have to feel comfortable in order to work and in order to move with a lot of freedom. Comfort gives you knowledge. It's good to learn, know, and later handle this knowledge comfortably.

440 ACKNOWLEDGEMENT. In my case, I think the best praise is my own. But it's praise that I haven't achieved yet. I always have a feeling of frustration–the feeling that the next collection is going to be the one to really show what I want to. It's utopian and futile, but that's how it works for me.

441 INSPIRATION. I will start a collection once I have decided the inspiration and theme for the collection. I like to research and fully develop the inspiration. This is one of my favorite and most exciting moments (the research and the discovery process). There have been different themes and inspirations for the collections over the years such as: Moroccan tiles, the Byzantine cross, the Russian group, Henry Matisse, a dragonfly, the garden, Tony Duquette.

442 REFERENCES. Fantasy and form. This is always consistent when I design for a collection. I always like to design and keep the flow of ideas going based on the creative moment and the inspiration I am feeling. I always prefer to create the fantasy pieces of the collection first. Then I think about who is going to wear this garment and where she is going. I will then create the more functional side of the collection.

443 MANNEQUIN. I love to personally drape the fabrics on the form and/or on a live model. For me, fabric has its own language and is a great communicator.

444 DEVELOPING A COLLECTION. The concept of the collection is translated through the color, fabrics, and details that are consistent throughout.

445 MATERIALS. I choose the particular fabric based on how I envision the garment. I love working with a variety of fabrics such as matte jersey, matte laces, silk chiffons, and novelty fabrics. My fabrics are created for me in different parts of the world, i.e. France, Italy, and Switzerland.

© Gideon Lewin

Spring 06

JOANNA MASTROIANNI 230 WEST 38TH STREET 15TH FLOOR NEW YORK, NY 10018 212.764.0840

Women's Wear Daily • The Retailers' Daily News

WWDW

Inspirat
What's Turning Designers

"Renowned for her use of hand-beading and body-conscious silhouettes, Mastroianni's flirtatious fall 2005 collection has a modern edge inspired by the details of the French Art Deco of the Thirties." — Joanna Mastroianni

Christina Ricci

Women's Wear Daily
April 11, 2006

446 IS FASHION ART? Creating a beautiful garment is an art form. I feel it is my responsibility as a creative creature to design something of beauty that makes the wearer feel good about themselves when they are wearing it. I see clothing as works of art that should be collected.

447 COLORS. Color for me is the messenger. It should complement the lines of the silhouette and sometimes it can dictate the silhouette. It is the first thing that one will notice about a garment. There are certain colors that are consistent in every one of my collections (black, of course).

448 COMMUNICATION. Communication is incredibly important all the time. You work with a team of people that you must direct and guide so that they can help in the creation of the idea that has developed in your brain. As a designer, you will usually be the first to have that vision. That also comes with responsibility and the need for follow-through until its full completion (I refer to this as the creative journey of the garment).

449 EVOLUTION. I always feel the need to improve every day and every hour as I journey through the creative process and life.

450 ADVICE. Be passionate and thrilled to have the gift and the desire to create. Challenge your creativity on a daily basis (do not settle). Always respect the art form that it is. Spend more time developing and sculpting with fabrics and techniques. Learn the rules and the engineering of garments. Once you know them really well, try breaking them so that you never stop experimenting. Always have fun.

045

Joanna Mastroianni
www.joannamastroianni.com

Joanna Mastroianni presented her first collection 15 years ago with a clear vision of its time. As the years have passed, Joanna has been designing clothes that uphold this quality and reflect her innate ability to capture the current pulse of fashion. Her inspiration comes from a variety of things, such as Moroccan mosaics, Matisse, or a dragonfly, which give rise to collections that are part fantasy–her favorite part–and part function. The most characteristic features of her pieces are their clean and sensual lines, and the versatility and elegance with which a dress for a pin-up girl can become one for a damsel out of the Middle Ages. Her designs are typically seen at Oscar, Tony, and Grammy award ceremonies, being worn by stars such as Sharon Stone, Jane Seymour, Angela Bassett, and Tara Reid.

046

Juan Vidal
www.juanvidaldesign.com

Juan Vidal's grandfather, great-grandfather, and great-great-grandfather were tailors, and his mother was the manageress of a boutique. So much influence from fashion and image at first intimidated the Spaniard, who chose to study fine arts, seeking his means of expressing aesthetic taste in painting. However, his taste for fashion was able to overcome his fear of not living up to his prestigious family and he enrolled in the Felicidad Duce Fashion School in Barcelona. In 2005, he won the ModaFAD Award for the Best Collection, which opened the doors of Bread & Butter to him. Since then, he has presented his collections on different Spanish runways each season. He has no specific references when he designs. He likes to think of women as something intangible and femininity as having a multitude of forms, and would like to dress all of them.

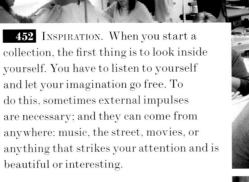

451

WORKPLACE. It's important to have your own space, a place where you can lose yourself, by yourself, with your music, images, and movies. My most important tool is a small notebook for sketching that I always carry with me. My first ideas come from there. I like to think first and develop the idea later. The atelier is where you fight, and where you see yourself working.

452 INSPIRATION. When you start a collection, the first thing is to look inside yourself. You have to listen to yourself and let your imagination go free. To do this, sometimes external impulses are necessary; and they can come from anywhere: music, the street, movies, or anything that strikes your attention and is beautiful or interesting.

453 MUSES. I'm influenced by the female figures that surround me. I also like to imagine, like in the movies, different female archetypes, and play with them; mix them up. The past is also a great reference. Fashion has a cultural side to it. The more you see, the more you learn; and the more you learn, the more you develop.

454 DEVELOPING A COLLECTION. I prefer that the concept behind the collection imbue everything through the design of the look and in a very subtle way. I believe that when something is too faithful to the idea it originates from, it loses its mystery and becomes something obvious.

455 MATERIALS. It's necessary to know the raw materials and how to use them; although sometimes you can use a cloth the wrong way and come out with new results. Before designing a single garment, I like to have practically all of the fabrics on the table. I'm not one of those people that say "never" and I'm even less so in fashion. The fabrics you detest today could be your masterpiece tomorrow.

456 COLORS. Sometimes you want to do something new; at other times you want to mix, while at others you want everything to be in the same shade. Depending on how you apply these three ideas about color, you come up with one result or another.

457 TRADITIONAL MANUFACTURING VS. EXPERIMENTATION. I think the ideal thing is to have enough knowledge of tradition so as to be able to experiment. You need a base; there's no evolution without a prior culture.

458 EVOLUTION. Collection after collection, I try to keep the sophistication and sensuality, but with a different wrapping. It's like a wolf in sheep's clothing: it will always be a wolf, but it has fun with what it's wearing.

459 CHALLENGE. I definitely feel that I have to exceed myself every six months; each season is like a public examination. It makes you want to grow and learn. You want more each time, so you have to offer more.

460 ACKNOWLEDGEMENT. The best applause is personal; you have to applaud yourself by yourself. I still haven't been able to. It depends on how demanding you are. I'm very grateful for the response I get from the public; but often some things are left unsaid. I always say that to be a young designer is to do what you can and not always what you want.

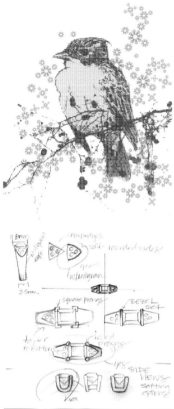

461 INSPIRATION. The themes and sensations go hand in hand. As a designer, you have to pay a lot of attention to your state of mind when you design because it comes to the surface in the themes.

462 REFERENCES. I generally find inspiration in something I have seen that has made an impact on me. I'm inspired by artwork, a beautiful bird, a crowded street, a pretty landscape, etc.

463 WORKPLACE. First I draw a sketch in any of the notebooks that I always have with me; then I take it to my work table and we analyze the size, weight, type of process, whether it should be cast or die cut. The piece changes totally depending on the process involved. It is very important to analyze the process each piece of jewelry needs, because this is the guarantee of good workmanship, good weight, and good finishing that will finally be reflected in the point of sale.

464 DEVELOPING A COLLECTION. For the concept of the collection we must take several factors into account and analyze world trends carefully. We should not go against them if we want our products to be commercial. We must take into account colors, shapes, materials, and, most important of all, a theme. This, together with fieldwork and intuition, is fused to bring about my designs.

465
MATERIALS. Materials generally used in jewelry are gold, silver, copper, and brass. This is where the science of a good designer comes in. Good creativity is searching for a blend of these materials with other, more alternative materials, such as leather, cord, fabrics, synthetics, natural materials, etc. I try not to use synthetic materials because my brand is particularly known for featuring materials of high-quality jewelry, offering exclusive and novel designs.

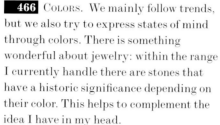

466 COLORS. We mainly follow trends, but we also try to express states of mind through colors. There is something wonderful about jewelry: within the range I currently handle there are stones that have a historic significance depending on their color. This helps to complement the idea I have in my head.

467 TRADITIONAL MANUFACTURING VS. EXPERIMENTATION. I like to mix tradition with experimentation because, although I'm a woman on the cutting edge, I have deep-rooted traditions. I think the mixture of the two is ideal. Whenever I design something I think about whether I would wear it or not.

468 YOUR RIGHT ARM? My right arm is Mejía, the person who knows how to interpret my work to perfection. She is capable of conveying each need to jewelers. She makes for perfect symbiosis!

469 INDIVIDUALITY VS. GROUP BELONGING. My brand makes people wearing it feel different; they feel they can wear a very avant-garde accessory to a very elegant party and then use the same accessory the next day with a pair of jeans and a T-shirt.

470 BRAND VALUES. My label promises that someone buying something from Juanita Álvarez will feel very comfortable and genuine; it promises looks and, more importantly, being set apart from the rest.

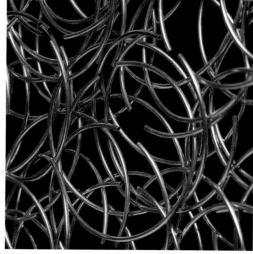

047

Juanita Álvarez
www.juanitalvarez.com

Juanita Álvarez studied at the Rome Institute of Design, finishing her studies in 1995. Under the supervision of renowned Italian jeweler, Renato Piva, she worked extensively to evolve her style and the production process of her work. When she returned to Colombia, she launched her own sophisticated jewelry line, balancing materials including gold and precious gemstones in beautifully refined designs. They have been offered in the national and international markets since the early 2000s. Her invitation and participation to this year's Bread & Butter Barcelona is a further validation of her success. She presented her latest collection "Érase una vez" (Once Upon a Time). She repeated in Paris at the Bijorhca Expo with "Bon Voyage," a collection of her work from the last two years made of silver and copper.

048

Junko Shimada
www.junkoshimada.com

After her design studies at the Sujino Gajen Dressmaker Institute of Tokyo, Junko Shimada visited Paris and, being seduced by the city, decided to stay. This was in the late sixties and Junko Shimada was one of the first Japanese designers to settle in Paris. After having worked in the Mafia Design Studio she entered Cacharel first as Chief Designer of childrens' wear, then of menswear for six years. Junko Shimada created her own design studio in 1981 and within just a few years she was being celebrated by the press as the "most Parisian Japanese." She opened her first boutique in the city in 1984 on rue Étienne Marcel. She has about 20 exclusive shops for her main line and she creates luggage, glasses, scarves, kimonos, and golf wear under several licensed brands.

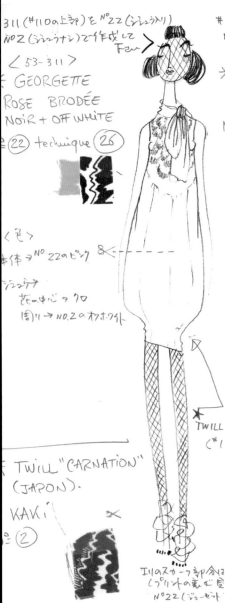

471 INSPIRATION. I don't think of one thing in particular when starting a collection. The life around us is inspiration in itself–a person in the street, a film, art, music. First is the vision of the collection; then the reflection on that vision.

472 MUSES. The silhouette of the collection comes from the attitude of the woman that I draw, something determined by the posture. And from that gesture, the volumes and proportions of the collection take life. Along with the general attitude, there are two main juxtaposing ideas that determine in which direction the collection will go.

473 BRAND VALUES. Junko Shimada is individuality in the domain of sophisticated, luxury, trash, bourgeois, glamour.

474 MATERIALS. It goes with the attitude of the collection. I buy fabrics from all over the world: Japan, Italy, France, Australia, Switzerland. I choose according to quality and directly from the suppliers.

475 MISSION. Stay true and honest to yourself. Liberty in creation. This brings respect for your vision and integrity.

476 STYLE. Sexy-fresh-cute-sassy with a certain degree of innocence. There is a deeper, serious side that plays with the innocent side. A juxtaposition of innocence and seriousness comes in and out of the style.

477 SALES. Think about who you design for, know your market. I take these into consideration but it does not influence my creativity.

478 ACKNOWLEDGEMENT. When people have understood your work.

479 COMMUNICATION. Is the key to everything. We have a fashion press office in Paris that handles our strategies.

480 GOOD HABITS. Modesty is most important, then to be exigent/demanding with yourself, to persevere, and to be curious.

© Alfredo Piola

481 INSPIRATION. You have to be open to inspiration coming from anywhere and you have to allow yourself that time for soaking up the world around you. Be open to possibilities. Inspiration can come from anywhere—an antique, a piece of fabric, an old TV series, people you know, as well as simply not being able to find something in your wardrobe that you think you should have.

482 WORKPLACE. We have three or four different fit models and while they have slightly different body shapes what they have in common is that they're all Karen Walker girls and they're all interesting and have natural style. When we cast for fit models the actual measurements are secondary to their personal style and personality. We have fit sessions two or three times a week during our intense design times and we have a studio set up in the design room where we photograph every look on, comment during the fitting, but also make additional comments after reviewing the photos later.

483 TRADITIONAL MANUFACTURING VS. EXPERIMENTATION. Our making is based on traditional techniques, however, we embrace all new technology with enthusiasm and have the two working alongside one another. It's the attitude of the product that makes it modern, not its methods.

484 BRAND VALUES. Creativity.

485
COLORS. The color has to fit with what it is you're trying to communicate. It's what sets the mood, it's like the music in a movie.

486 COMMUNICATION STRATEGY. Creativity is our message and our communication strategy is surprise and spontaneity.

487 STYLE. We retain our sense of humor and the desire to make believable clothes.

488 IS FASHION ART? We love art and we make clothes.

489 ADVICE. You're never ready so just get on with it.

490 SALES. Good sales come from making clothes that are uplifting and inspire people to wear them.

© Derek Henderson

049

Karen Walker
www.karenwalker.com

Karen Walker is a New Zealand-born fashion designer with a reputation for her original, effortless, and unpretentious style. Since 2002 Karen has been working closely with stylist Heathermary Jackson on all her collections. In addition to her main womenswear collections, Karen also designs Karen Walker Jewelry, Karen Walker Eyewear, and Karen Walker Paints, a selection of paint colors sold through Resene paint stores. Celebrities such as Björk, Sienna Miller, Jennifer Lopez, Claire Danes, Cate Blanchett, Liv Tyler, Mandi Moore, Shirley Manson, Kate Hudson, Kelly Osbourne, Claudia Schiffer, Drew Barrymore, and Madonna all favor her work with four pieces from the Dust collection featured on Kate Winslet in Michel Gondry and Charlie Kaufmanís' legendary movie *Eternal Sunshine of the Spotless Mind.*

050

Kathleen König/Haltbar
www.haltbar.de

The German word *haltbar* translates as durable, solid, and lasting, which perfectly describes the spirit of this label. Since its foundation in 2001, the company has been innovating and reinterpreting classic German fashion. Their philosophy is to work with small family businesses in order to preserve existing infrastructure, know-how, and heritage. Haltbar started producing and distributing a line of interior, accessory, and textiles up until 2003 when the side project Haltbar Murkudis was born. Along with Kostas Murkudis, a unisex collection based on German workwear was produced and marketed. Through its distributors and its flagship store in Munich, Haltbar sells solid materials, often with handmade elements that are resistant to fading and wear and tear, in an effort to become timeless and a favorite for basics.

©Thomas Degen

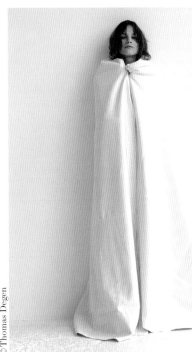

© Thomas Degen

© Markus Strasser

© Markus Jans

© Markus Jans

© Thomas Degen

491 INSPIRATION. My label provides me with a frame and then I just keep my eyes, my ears, and my mind open.

492 WORKPLACE. My atelier is situated in a nice Munich neighborhood that borders on a historical graveyard where many famous artists, like Klenze, are buried. I really believe this atmosphere makes for fantastic vibes.

493 MATERIALS. My label is called Haltbar ("durability"). That is why I look for old workwear fabrics or draperies from small weaving mills, mostly from Germany, Switzerland, and Austria.

494 COLORS. Use colors to enhance your designs. To me, color follows function.

495 DEVELOPING A COLLECTION. Try to think what you like and then go from there. To me, functionality, simplicity, and my philosophy are key.

©Thomas Degen

496 INDIVIDUALITY VS. GROUP BELONGING. Individuality. Definitely.

497 STYLE. I want my clothes to feel natural and I communicate this to my costumers. Other than that, I feel that clothes don't need a strategy.

498 EVOLUTION. Distinctiveness, articulateness, simplicity, self-evidence. The one thing I do change is accessories.

499 ADVICE. Be consequent. Then stick to it. Be passionate. And always brush your teeth.

500 SALES. You never know, let them surprise you. But make sure you have a completed picture in your collection.

502 REFERENCES. My mother is a wholesaler of Italian fashion. When I was a child she would let me play at making displays. I would travel to Italy with her and help her at trade fairs. I suppose having this subconscious is what made me decide to go into fashion when I finished school.

503 DEVELOPING A COLLECTION. I mix aspects of Spanish suburban *barrio* culture, sport, hip-hop, and luxury.

504 COMMUNICATION. It happens the same way. We present our projects to the public on two platforms: at BBB on an international fair level with consolidated brands and at 080 at an alternative showroom level, with a runway show among young international designers. It's useful as long as the showroom is right for your label and the clients that visit it, too.

505 CHALLENGES. Moving forward with what I've learned.

501
STYLE. I define my style as "sport deluxe," a mish-mash of what is considered street, suburban, and urban culture on the one hand with their opposites: luxury, power, kitsch...all mixed in with rap, hip-hop, and trashiness.

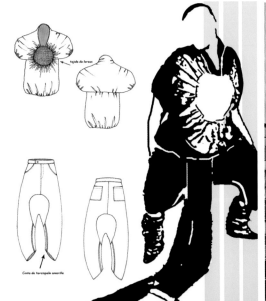

Krizia Robustella official store.

506 SALES. After presenting at the Cibeles runway show, and creating a label and seeing how difficult it is for young designers to sell in multi-brand stores, I decided to open an outlet of my own with my mother's help, seeing as the retail space belonged to her. It hasn't been easy, and still isn't. Knock on wood.

507 ACKNOWLEDGEMENT. Since my first collection in the Ego show during Cibeles fashion week, I've had very good acceptance. Whenever the word "tracksuit" was mentioned anywhere, my name was on it.

508 BRAND VALUES. My collections are not exclusively directed at followers of rap. I believe you have to define your label and have your own values, but that doesn't mean cutting yourself off. My label is focused on a public that is young in spirit, daring, non-conformist, and with a sense of humor.

509 ADVICE. I don't normally do special things clients ask for; I like to focus on my collections, and I don't like going off the track by doing work that doesn't fit my style.

510 TEAMWORK. I always manage to get someone to help me with styling for photo shoots and runways...I'm pretty bad at all that.

051

Krizia Robustella
www.kriziarobustella.com

When she was a child, Krizia moved from her native Amsterdam to Barcelona, where she still lives. She studied fashion design at the Felicidad Duce Design and Fashion College, where she won the prize for best collection in her final year. She was also invited to take part in Projecte Bressol, a project to assist and train young fashion designers organized by the regional government of Catalonia. Defined by Krizia Robustella as "sport deluxe," the designer takes sports clothing of the last few decades to create a world of her own where comfort blends with luxury through the forms and fabrics that she had been setting aside for formal wear. Hers is a label for eccentric types who like to take risks and need to be seen during the day, without losing the glamour and elegance that typify nights in the big city.

© Dizy Diaz

052

Lambert Perera Cortés, Sibylle Genin/Baron Baronne
www.baronbaronne.com

Frenchwoman Sibylle Genin and Catalan Lambert Perera Cortés met in Paris while studying at the prestigious École de la Chambre Syndicale de la Couture Parisien. When they finished their studies, they decided to join forces on this project which has now made a name for itself. Baron Baronne is based in Paris and produced in Andorra. Since their first collection in 2007, the concept that defines the label was made very clear: the fine line between feminine and masculine. They have since been flirting with the type of clothes that result from giving a masculine feel to feminine pieces. The aim of the label is to rid people of their complexes and offer them a young and innovative product without restriction that can be used for every occasion.

511 INSPIRATION. To start a collection we establish a theme that we use for research, and then one idea comes after another. In the end, we work not only one theme but all different ideas that became connected.

512 MUSES. We try to design modern, original, and comfortable clothes that are convenient to everyone. This is our drive and why we do not have any muse. Our place where we work is a laboratory of ideas born from our research.

513 DEVELOPING A COLLECTION. Every piece is a personal process made unique by analyzing the pattern and changing the volume of its shape until we approve its look. Then we choose the color assembly and add details.

514 COLORS. We use quite basic colors–blue and black–and add colors we choose from Première Vision tendencies. Our personal inspiration for colors comes from art exhibitions (for example Erwin Olaf, whome we just saw at the Neerlandais Institute in Paris), architecture, traveling, nature, and observing street life. Moreover, something quite funny, but old people's style is very interesting–the way they wear their clothes and the color association.

515 TRADITIONAL MANUFACTURING VS. EXPERIMENTATION. Both. We base our work on what is classic and traditional; we then add the modernity, the innovation. The tradition and experimentation are connected–there are no borders. We need representative products and it is necessary to adapt to the demand. The customer asks for a portable but innovative product all at once, and it therefore becomes necessary to adapt ourselves and organize both to correspond to this demand.

516 INDIVIDUALITY VS. GROUP BELONGING. Our creations are more individualistic. We try to work out new ways of designing clothes. Our goal is to find individuality again in the crowd so that a person can distance himself from a group and not the opposite. The difference is to carry both novelty and modernity.

517 COMMUNICATION. Communication is always important. We do a lot of our communicating through the Internet. We work on it. We are not divided up into a single type of communication nor are we like others who have so many effects, such as short-lived selling organizations. Yet, we are able to present our brand just as well as the other creators. And sometimes it is enough to have a meeting and some word of mouth to get established.

518 STREET FASHION VS. FASHION DESIGNER. Fashion comes from both; one does not go without the other. We are inspired by what we see in the street and the street is inspired by certain tendencies of designers. There is continual inspiration.

519 GOOD HABITS. *Rigueur, créativité,* modernity, visionary being.

520 SALES. It is important to create an innovative product but also a product that can be worn. In our collection, we use creative cloths. And though we use less of them in more commercial items, it does not directly influence our creativity.

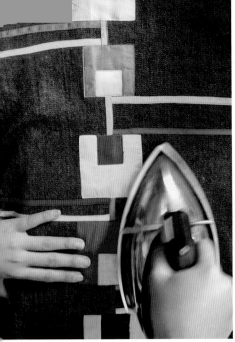

521 INSPIRATION. We always prefer to have a theme when starting a collection. It can be an abstract or geometric theme, like a circle, or a figurative one, like animals. We always understand collections to be somewhat open to being worked on, not only during the launch period, which is why we like more general and timeless themes that can be taken up again after the first burst of energy. Naturally, daily life in the streets of Hanoi is a constant source of inspiration.

522 REFERENCES. We have in mind the chula client, who is someone willing to take a chance on something different, but not outlandish.

523 MATERIALS. We work a lot with parallel material that is not directly related to fashion: photos, abstract painting, architecture, graphic design, images of public figures, lots of Google images. We like to think of making clothes like making a meal–you want to cook and so you go to the market to find fresh produce that is in season. We are lucky that there are good fabric markets in Hanoi that move with the seasons, which isn't very functional for pre-producing orders, but it is a lot of fun. Clearly, the star product in Vietnam is silk in its different textures, and in an unbelievable variety of colors. If you have the best ingredients, why not cook with them? We haven't said no to any material.

524 INDIVIDUALITY VS. GROUP BELONGING. People feel different in our clothes, especially because of the limited production runs for each piece and the personal attention we try to give to our clients.

525
COLOR. You can't understand chula without color; or better yet, without colors. We have attempted to make an outfit in a single color but we haven't succeeded. Clothes are an excuse for working with color.

© Pedro Spoggi

526 STYLE. Chula mainly makes women's clothes and generally for special occasions. The most common response our clients give to us is that many men (who are not particularly interested in fashion) approach them to say they like their outfit very much.

527 PHILOSOPHY. Our message is that you can dress elegantly but with a sense of humor. Of course in such a uniform world you can still find unique pieces at a reasonable price and in direct contact with the designers.

528 EVOLUTION. We don't follow the pace set by six-month runway shows and collections. When you're starting out in the business, it's murder keeping up with the big labels. We tend to start two collections each season. Right now we're working on a somewhat figurative animal collection, and on a more abstract one with the triangle as its leitmotif. But at the same time we are revisiting the collections from the last three years.

529 IS FASHION ART? One day we were with a client in our atelier and she suddenly saw an outfit one size smaller than hers which she fell in love with. We offered to make it to measure, but she bought it, despite it not fitting her. She said she didn't want to wear it; she was going to frame it and hang it in her living room. This is only a story, but the truth is that when members of the public buy dress clothes, they're looking for more than just something to wear or a designer label.

530 GOOD HABITS. It's good not to shut yourself up in the design world: the magazines, the runway shows...

053

Laura Fontán, Diego Cortizas/chula
www.chula.es

Founded in Spain but based in Vietnam for two years now, chula is a clothing label created by designer Laura Fontán and architect Diego Cortizas. The company's dresses and coats combine the brightest colors from the world of Spanish design with the richness of Asian fabrics and manual embroidery techniques. Each garment is handcrafted, and finds exclusivity in the color variations, embroidery techniques, and pattern geometry. Collections are not designed according to the winter-summer rules–if it's winter in New York, it's summer in Cape Town, isn't it?–they are classified by theme. The label's limited production is sold in boutiques around the world including Madrid, Barcelona, Hanoi, Kuala Lumpur, Kuwait, Canberra, Luang Prabang, Graz, and Tokyo.

© Gonçalo Gaioso

054

Lidija Kolovrat
www.kolovratconcept.com

Bosnian-born artist, designer, healer, and teacher, Lidija Kolovrat, has been based since 1990 in Lisbon, Portugal. Her local studio is the platform for sale, research, work, and discoveries. Working womenswear and accessories since her early years in Zagreb, Lidija started showing her first entire menswear collection in March 2006 at Lisbon Fashion Week. With a strong, innovative, and crashing vision, her menswear has been around now for years. She has a multidisciplinary approach to her work, taking everything from the particular to the whole, observing everything in its entirety. In her words, design follows the inherent nature that goes, flows, and talks in objects. She regards fashion as a field where one can express and melt art, politics, human behavior, and social need.

© Patricia de Melo Moreira

© Alexander Koch

531 INSPIRATION. Before I start the collection, I recognize my feelings—that is the initial start of any reasoning. It is therefore more like a sensation from which the themes and sensations come out of organically.

532 DEVELOPING A COLLECTION. Because things start from initial reason-feeling, everything that gets developed falls into a place or it's eliminated.

533 COLORS. It is like a melody. It tunes the light. Therefore it can be lighter or heavier. Again, it is something intuitive, it comes to express the same feeling or take away from the initial idea and use it as a contrast.

534 BRAND VALUES. I promise research and constant appreciation.

535 INDIVIDUALITY VS. GROUP BELONGING. I pretty much defend freedom and, therefore, individuality. I work from that point. It is also very interesting to find and use common sense. These two ideas are not necessarily opposite. Just through the matter of liking them or not, I can decide between perspectives: individual or group belonging.

© Patricia de Melo Moreira

© Patricia de Melo Moreira

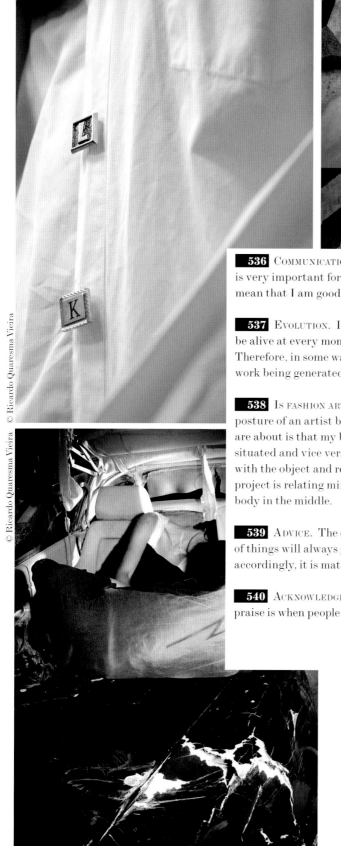

© Ricardo Quaresma Vieira

© Ricardo Quaresma Vieira

© Patricia de Melo Moreira

536 COMMUNICATION. Communication is very important for me, but that does not mean that I am good at it.

537 EVOLUTION. I feel that I need to be alive at every moment and to interact. Therefore, in some way there is always work being generated.

538 IS FASHION ART? I think I have the posture of an artist but what my exercises are about is that my body is mind-need situated and vice versa, as well as body with the object and reverse. My latest project is relating mind and space with the body in the middle.

539 ADVICE. The original feeling of things will always give the result accordingly, it is mathematical.

540 ACKNOWLEDGEMENT. The best praise is when people love my work!

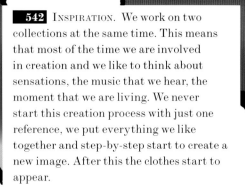

© Fernanda Calfat

541
GOOD HABITS. Don't worry about trends and the market. Stretch beyond the superficial and become more authentic.

542 INSPIRATION. We work on two collections at the same time. This means that most of the time we are involved in creation and we like to think about sensations, the music that we hear, the moment that we are living. We never start this creation process with just one reference, we put everything we like together and step-by-step start to create a new image. After this the clothes start to appear.

543 COLORS. We think any color goes with any other color...always! So, our biggest worry is about creating happy and colorful clothes to cause the same kind of feeling in the people that see them. We try making different shapes or prints, simply because we like it this way and this is our best motivation. Without it, everything becomes boring.

544 EVOLUTION. We feel the necessity to improve ourselves, to get up all the time. With every collection we dedicate a lot of energy and time to be better than the last one, being careful with each piece–remaking the prints ten times if necessary and starting the piece over again and again.

545 COMMUNICATION STRATEGY. We never thought about one communication strategy, but we always worry about our job's image. We have always loved beautiful images and we like to do this. Almost intuitively we create a strong identity, starting from our name, Amonstro. We haven't worried about following the rules, and this became a point of difference.

546 STYLE. Individuality is always enduring and everyday it has more value. You lose the liberty of creation if you turn the focus entirely to business. We believe that when you start to worry about prices and what is current in fashion, your creativity becomes blocked.

547 TRADITIONAL MANUFACTURING VS. EXPERIMENTATION. Our job's base is in experimentation. We think about every part of the process and try new techniques, new ways to do things. The result sometimes is not what we expect but can surprise us, and this is great.

548 WORKPLACE. When we started to look for a place to be our atelier, we took one year to find the house. This is very important for us: the place that we work has to have good energy and life–plenty of light with lots of plants and all of our books and magazines.

549 ADVICE. You cannot be superficial!

550 ACKNOWLEDGEMENT. Create beautiful images.

055

Lívia Torres, Helena Pimenta/Amonstro
www.amonstro.com.br

Lívia Torres and Helena Pimenta founded the company in 2002. In 2007 they opened their first store and showroom. With remarkable character, the two stylists complete each other–giving way to Amonstro, a unique and strong personality. The exclusive print work often features animal designs done by in-house and guest illustrators. The first T-shirts were created in partnership with the illustrator Lovefoxxx, also vocalist of the band CSS. Immediately after, they were called to design Ellus Second Floor's F/W 04 collection. After this breakthrough, they have always been invited to participate to the Amni HotSpot. Their other creative outlets are a collection of cloth animals alongside artist Lala Martinez Corrêa and cover design of the book *Monstro* along with 25 other Brazilian artists.

© Jochen Arndt

056

Livia Ximénez-Carrillo, Christine Pluess/mongrels in common
www.mongrelsincommon.com

Mongrels in common are based in Berlin-Mitte, Germany. They made their debut at the Moët et Chandon Fashion Award 2006, showing S/S 07 containing menswear and womenswear. With their first collection at premium exhibitions in Berlin, they won the Premium Young Designers Award for best menswear F/W 06/07. In 2007 they were nominated for the German New Faces Award. Uncompromisingly mixing masculine severity and straightness with female delicacy combined with high-quality materials, they present a look that is elegant and exclusive as well as sexy and cool. Designers Livia Ximénez-Carrillo and Christine Pluess constantly aim for a break of style by combining masculine and feminine elements, coupling avant-garde design with a casual, classical style, and by combining subdued with flamboyant colors.

551 INSPIRATION. In every collection we unite two opposite cultures. Since the two of us are mongrels, meaning we are both from multicultural backgrounds, it is the closest thing for us to do. It represents our personalities. For instance, in the latest F/W 09/10 collection we unite the rough charm of contemporary art in Berlin and influences of the futuristic and graphic architecture of Dubai.

552 DEVELOPING A COLLECTION. Our work approach is different from many other designers. We rarely draw our designs, we discuss fashion and drape a lot.

553 MATERIALS. We made it very clear from the beginning what target group we are aiming at. Hence we only choose high-quality fabrics. It's essential to regularly go to the Fabric Fair Première Vision in Paris in order to meet fabric manufacturers and to be informed about new trends and color charts.

554 YOUR RIGHT ARM? Stephanie, our assistant. She's the best!

555 BRAND VALUES. High-quality fabrics and high-quality manufacturing for a reasonable high price.

557 COMMUNICATION. Communication is definitely interlinked with sales. We have been working with a renowned press agency since the beginning and it has always been a great help. Many of our customers came to us after having seen an article about us or an editorial with our fashion.

558 STREET FASHION VS. FASHION DESIGNER. The best would be a mix of both. Everyone is obviously influenced by what one sees on the streets, but then it is not a matter of copying what you see but reinventing and further developing a trend into a new design.

559 ADVICE. To set the priorities right, especially in moments of enormous stress, in order to guarantee that you'll be on time.

560 SALES. It is always important that a garment looks good on the body and that it can actually be worn. Since we have to live on our fashion we want to sell and therefore we have to make some compromises not only in the design but also in the way a piece is produced. If it's too difficult to produce, the costs will rise and then a piece becomes too expensive and no one will buy it.

556
EVOLUTION. With every new collection we try to top the last one. Once a collection is finished you always find things that could have been done better and we try to incorporate these ideas into the new collection.

561 INSPIRATION. We tend to think of themes related to movies, architecture, music, books we've read, old family photos, souvenirs, and more. We're interested in transmitting the feelings these familiar things produce in us; they are the things that inspire us.

562 DEVELOPING A COLLECTION. We decide on the leitmotif and we convey it through volume, lines, colors, and fabrics. In this way, we give each piece the common denominator of the collection. For example, the 2009 summer collection was inspired by a journey to the jungle in the fifties. We chose linens and cottons to give a sense of coolness. We added volume with puckering reminiscent of that time. For the men's line, we used the typical stripes from that decade, safari suits, mosquito nets, etc.

563 MATERIALS. I choose them intuitively; but we always look for high quality and natural fabrics. I tend to fall in love at first sight with prints and embroidery, although we sometimes have them made to our design. We buy them in fairs, from sales reps, wholesalers, and in Europe, India, Japan, and America. We

always take advantage of our trips to buy. What we never use are synthetic fabrics. We always imagine someone on a plane for eight or maybe ten hours in a synthetic garment–the smell wouldn't be very pleasant. We don't normally work with technical fabrics, but we're not against them.

564 TRADITIONAL MANUFACTURING VS. EXPERIMENTATION. A mixture of the two. We like to experiment, but always over a perfect base of patternmaking, knowledge of fabrics, and perfect finishing in sewing. All this, which seems to be more traditional, helps the result of the experiment to have quality.

565 INDIVIDUALITY VS. GROUP BELONGING. Our clothes make people feel different and as each garment isn't produced in large runs, it would be difficult for buyers to find half the city in the same shirt. Also, our target market tends to be bohemian bourgeois, *bobos*, who understand our concept of fashion owing to their philosophy, although we are increasingly surprised by the variety of people wearing our clothes.

© Alter Ego Magazine

566 EVOLUTION. We change the theme of the collection each season, but we keep many of the strong points that are the signature of the house: versatility of the pieces, a timeless look, a small touch of retro, quality finishing and manufacturing, and a mixture of fabrics and colors. One theme we like a lot lately is to create items that don't die with each collection; they aren't repeated, but are given a new version. A single garment can be given changes in the next collection through color, cut, and volume.

567 IS FASHION ART? Art provides pleasure. Fashion, in a way, does too but we also want to make it functional for daily life, not just decorative. It was born to cover a need, and it has evolved greatly, but its main function should be usefulness.

568 SALES. In order to sell, you have to make the concept reach clients easily and with strength so they understand it, buy it, and wear it. It's a great deal of pressure, which is why so many collections tend to have basic or dark pieces. In the end, they are clothes with guaranteed sales. It's very dangerous to fall into that trap, particularly when you're supposed to be marking a difference.

569 COMMUNICATION. We give great importance to this, especially the visual side. We do a lot of work with the image of each campaign together with our style team. We control the label's publicity and we have our own pressroom.

570
TRAINING. Besides our training, our best lessons were learned setting up our business. Each day is a constant lesson in patternmaking, cutting, accounting, styling, press, consultations and visits to clients, psychology, sales, management, photography, window-dressing, graphic design, and purchasing. All of this comes from setting up a company. It is a huge responsibility, but it also gives you great freedom to design and decide by yourself.

057

Llamazares y de Delgado
www.llamazaresydedelgado.com

Fabricio Pérez Martínez and Jaime Martínez Llamazares form Llamazares y de Delgado. They presented their first collection in 1998. The sensation of their show and the exceptional press feedback launched them in creating two prêt-couture collections each year ever since. Their design is focused mainly on garment versatility, which allows the items to be easily combined with the most various and daring combinations of colors and fabrics. Lush details from the exotic Far East and a revised "New Look" spirit come together in Llamazares y de Delgado's decorative wear. The Himalayas, a yurt where caravan pass the night surrounded by silks, spices, furs, brocades, kilims, and the spiraling smoke of burning incense mix with the sensuality and femininity of "New Look" Paris 1948, are all part of their mysterious yet chic style.

058

Louise Amstrup
www.louise-amstrup.com

Danish-born Louise Amstrup spent part of her childhood living in Germany to then return and complete her studies. In 2003 she graduated from Akadamie Modedesign, where she was awarded the Graduate Talent prize. Now based in London, Louise has worked with various designers including Alexander McQueen, Jonathan Saunders, Alistair Carr, Sofia Kokosalaki, and Catherine Walker. However, with the growing interest and demand for her work, she successfully launched her self-titled debut collection "Louise Amstrup" in 2006 and, following a phenomenal response, is proud to announce the launch of her third collection. Recently, Louise showcased her collections at London Fashion Week for two seasons, was awarded sponsorship through the Fashion Scout to show her S/S 09 collection at Shanghai Fashion Week, and opened Copenhagen Fashion Week with her F/W 09 collection.

SECTION FROM
A/W 09-10
MOOD BOARD

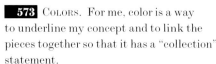

571 INSPIRATION. I usually start off by evaluating my previous collection and look at strengths and weaknesses. Then I start my research for the next collection. It often comes naturally to go in a different direction, inspiration-wise. For me, it is important to create something new yet still with my signature.

572 MATERIALS. I source my fabrics from all over the world. Personally, I love silks because they have a very luxurious feel and quality and yet come in so many variations that it never gets boring. It is "dangerous" to say never whenever it comes to creative work, but so far I have not worked with polyester satins or chiffons and they will not be a part of my next collection either.

573 COLORS. For me, color is a way to underline my concept and to link the pieces together so that it has a "collection" statement.

574 EVOLUTION. Yes! I think it is important to look at my career as a journey and development. I do my best every season, however as soon as a collection is done I think of how to improve and progress. This is what keeps the dynamic of a label.

575 STYLE. I am always very focused on maintaining a very high quality of the pieces as well as the design. I obviously also have some signature styles and features that you will see again—however always slightly changed and new. I do not think my style loses anything, however I do often decide to drop certain styles in order to strengthen my style overall.

© Mads Perch

© Mads Perch

© Mads Perch

577 GOOD HABITS. Apart from always keeping an open mind in terms of design, make sure you know how to do patterns and sewing on a very high standard yourself.

578 YOUR RIGHT ARM? My right arm is my assistant Cindy. She has been working for me for more than a year and it is great to have someone around who understands my "language." Not only is she technically really skilled but she also has a calm and lovely personality.

579 INDIVIDUALITY VS. GROUP BELONGING. I believe that fashion gives the person an opportunity to emphasize her individuality or emphasize a group belonging all depending on her wish, and isn't that the essence of democracy?

580 COMMUNICATION. Communication is essential! There is always a story or a message behind each collection and naturally it is important to try and get that across. This can be done in many ways and I guess that, being the designer behind the collection, it would be a mistake to leave all communication for someone else to do. However, I do work with a PR company and they are doing an amazing job, which I alone would never be able to do.

576 ADVICE. The best lesson I have ever received is that "cutting corners" never pays off. And that if you have the courage to give it your all then you have already come really far.

© Mads Perch

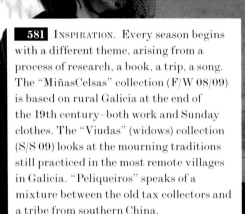

581 INSPIRATION. Every season begins with a different theme, arising from a process of research, a book, a trip, a song. The "MiñasCelsas" collection (F/W 08/09) is based on rural Galicia at the end of the 19th century—both work and Sunday clothes. The "Viudas" (widows) collection (S/S 09) looks at the mourning traditions still practiced in the most remote villages in Galicia. "Peliqueiros" speaks of a mixture between the old tax collectors and a tribe from southern China.

582 DEVELOPING A COLLECTION. Once the theme has been decided, I look for all of the information I can find and all of the crafted elements I can use. I start to sketch, to search for fabrics, to decide colors, and to embody my initial ideas in designs. Then I start to make patterns and create the clothes directly on the mannequin.

583 COLORS. The range of colors for a collection is set by the theme. Earth colors in "MiñasCelsas" represent the countryside, the dust, and age. For "Viudas" black is featured in all of its tones, from jet black to gray, to show the different stages of mourning. "Peliqueiros" has white to symbolize purity, while it uses gold for wealth. Red, blue, yellow, and green are the colors people used to parody the political regime of the time.

584 TRADITIONAL MANUFACTURING VS. EXPERIMENTATION. I prefer tradition. I research traditional elements for each collection: traditional Camariñas bobbin lace, embroidery made with pieces of jet, the crochet made by old women. I apply these traditional elements in an experimental way to achieve cutting-edge pieces.

585 BRAND VALUES. My clothes make people feel special. You have to escape from monotony and uniformity.

586 COMMUNICATION. I'm in charge of that at the moment. I can't afford the services of a PR company. The ideas for runway shows are all mine.

587 EVOLUTION. You have to do better with every collection, but it's something you have to work at every day. Collections overlap. You haven't finished one and you're already starting on the next. You're in a spiral with no end in sight.

588 IS FASHION ART? Fashion is my means of expression. Fashion is my life.

589 ACKNOWLEDGEMENT. The smile on people's faces is what keeps me going.

590
GOOD HABITS. Sleep is a waste of time. It's a difficult world and you have to work a lot. There are days when you lose complete track of time.

059

Manuel Bolaño
www.manuelbolano.com

This adopted son of Lugo returned to his birthplace of Barcelona to study at the Felicidad Duce Design and Fashion College. He presented his graduation collection in 2007 that was later shown successfully in Murcia, Bilbao, and Madrid. He returned to Barcelona for Bread & Butter where he was declared winner of the Felicidad Duce Award for Best Collection 06/07 and received the Young Talent Prize 07 presented by Bread & Butter Studio to the most innovative collection. In September 2007 he came first in Projecte Bressol, organized by the regional government of Catalonia, an achievement that marked his career taking off definitively in the world of fashion. Since then, it has been nothing but success and acclaim for him. He has already earned a permanent place in the Pasarela 080 runway shows held in Barcelona.

060

Marc Einsiedel, Julia Kleinwächter/Woolwill
www.woolwill.com

Marc Einsiedel studied graphic design at the University of Fine Arts Hamburg and finished his Master Studies in London. For many years he interested himself in street art as an artist and as a collector. Around 2006, he taught himself screen-printing, starting with an unconventional backyard workshop. When the first invitation to a young fashion show in Vienna occurred in September 2007, he teamed up with Julia, a communication design major at the University of Applied Sciences Hamburg. Together they designed, printed, and tailored the first collection. Receiving strong feedback, they decided to give other artists the possibility to make their artwork public using wearable textiles as canvases. That was the foundation to open a store with an integrated workshop. The Woolwill Store opened in June 2008, and has been flourishing ever since.

591
WORKPLACE. Our models are people we know and like, or the artists themselves. The studio inherits a very inspiring chaos, because of the many blank shirts and the manifold colors all over that stimulate our fantasies about new designs.

592 INSPIRATION. Each of our graphics has its own theme, yet we try to consider combinations of current colors and cuts, for example, at the collection with Superhorstjansen called "African Surf."

593 REFERENCES. We are trying to find the best mixture between the art we are actually influenced by, our own taste, and the taste of our customers.

594 MATERIALS. Woolwill's policy is to print on fair-trade and ecologically-manufactured clothes only, which naturally limits the sources. Plus, we have to select what cloth is suitable to print on and what is not.

595 TRADITIONAL MANUFACTURING VS. EXPERIMENTATION. Experimentation should be based on tradition/knowledge. Learn the rules first, then break them. A representative item can be helpful in terms of creating visual recognition value and therefore creating a brand.

596 YOUR RIGHT ARM? Our friends, especially Fiona Hinrichs and Patrick Ossen—our two permanent artists.

597 INDIVIDUALITY VS. GROUP BELONGING. Both. Individuality comes out of the handmade prints that turn every textile into a unicum. Group belonging comes in the form of the community of art collectors we invoke.

598 BRAND VALUES. Comfort, quality, a clear conscience, and a custom-made piece of art. Woolwill gives you the freedom to choose not only your own favorite shirt, sweater, hoody, etc., but also your favorite design from the current collection plus the color of both. One of our communication strategies is to make a vernissage for every new artist and his collection.

599 SALES. We always try to create a collection that both shows our creativity and pays the rent. Some designs are more mass-orientated while others are very personal and therefore not always easily accessible.

600 ACKNOWLEDGEMENT. That our customers regard themselves as "art collectors" and consider our clothes as artwork.

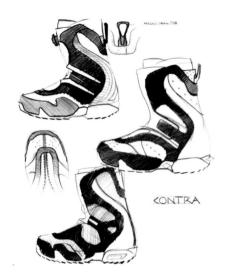

CONTRA

601 INSPIRATION. Every season the theme is the same: the brand. I look for opportunities to blend our identity into new products that the market can get excited about.

602 WORKPLACE. It is an open environment where designers can share ideas and points of view. No doors in the design department (headphones are a must at times). I like to have a table for the computer and a table for sketching–that requires a different mind-set.

603 ADVICE. Never give up pencil sketching. Creativity comes from using your hands.

604 MATERIALS. Finding materials durable enough for footwear can be challenging. We rely on our vendors to provide interesting choices at a good price. If there is something new we must have for the collection, our factories will look for a new material source. Never say never on a material. You really do not know what's going to look good in a few years time.

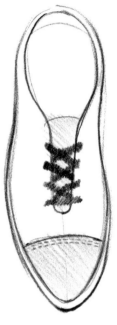

ROPE LACES

CYCLING PATTERN

605
TRADITIONAL MANUFACTURING VS. EXPERIMENTATION. As a designer, I prefer experimentation and the company prefers tradition. It is an interesting conflict but one that I enjoy. The product that results can be a nice blend of both. I am always trying to push the brand in subtle ways. We have room in the line for a statement piece but it is never a throw-away and must be a cornerstone in the line.

NO LACE OPTION = ELASTIC

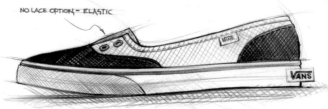

606 YOUR RIGHT ARM? The younger designers are always my right arm. I depend on them for their insight and closeness to the market.

607 COMMUNICATION. Staff meetings are important, but the vital communication comes out in the design reviews. It is a key part of the process where everything is open to debate and I can put my stamp on design direction.

608 BRAND VALUES. People who wear Vans want to be identified as someone that is a bit different. Vans promises originality, creativity, and authenticity at the core of action sports and youth culture. Having said that, I do like to make my designs simple, understandable, and accessible to everyone.

609 EVOLUTION. I used to go into every season thinking I needed to step up my design skills. Now I find myself wanting to improve my management skills and enjoying the design process more.

610 IS FASHION ART? Fashion is not art in the same sense as a painting or a sculpture. If you look at it like an automobile, where form and substance come together to make a beautiful object, then yes, it can be.

061

Mark Haskins/Vans
www.vans.com

Born in Laguna Beach, California, Mark Haskins started his career studying design at the Art Center College of Design in Pasadena, California. After working for Reebok designing soccer shoes for four years, he joined Vans in a move back to his native southern California. He now lives in Aliso Viejo with his wife Kristen and son Lars and, in a departure from action sports, he now enjoys triathlons. Mark has been with Vans for over ten years and he is currently the director of design for footwear and equipment. He combines managerial experience with passion and talent for shoe design. The overall concept of the shoe is what he seems to enjoy the most, with meticulous attention to detail. His designs always tend toward straightforwardness, ease of understanding, and accessibility.

062

Mark Liu
www.markliu.co.uk

Australian Mark Liu has always been interested in fashion, science, and philosophy. This was behind his graduation with honors with a fashion and textiles design degree from the University of Technology in Sydney. While writing his dissertation on innovative materials and new technologies in fashion, he found the idea of furthering his study of those concepts to be of great appeal. So he went to London, where he took an MA in design for textile futures. The fruit of these studies was his development of Zero Waste fashion, a technique to eliminate waste when cutting patterns. For this to happen, the rules of patternmaking needed to be torn up and reinvented. Zero Waste fashion had a successful debut at Esthetica, the space dedicated to sustainable fashion at London Fashion Week.

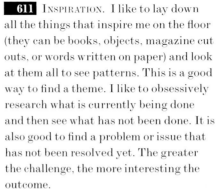

611 INSPIRATION. I like to lay down all the things that inspire me on the floor (they can be books, objects, magazine cut outs, or words written on paper) and look at them all to see patterns. This is a good way to find a theme. I like to obsessively research what is currently being done and then see what has not been done. It is also good to find a problem or issue that has not been resolved yet. The greater the challenge, the more interesting the outcome.

612 DEVELOPING A COLLECTION. The concept must become the thought process that creates each garment. It becomes predictable to cut and paste different themes from different time periods. I find it much more interesting to re-design the design process as part of the concept.

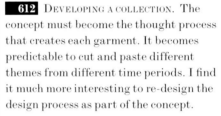

613 MATERIALS. I like to buy organic or alternative fabrics which are environmentally friendly. To do this you need to know exactly how and where they are made. It takes a lot of time and effort to trace the material from the fiber all the way to the final fabric. Sometimes I buy through textile agents and other times I am literally talking to the farmer who grows the animal or crop.

614 INDIVIDUALITY VS. GROUP BELONGING. Creations invoke different responses depending on who is wearing them. Their personality will determine individuality or group mentality.

615
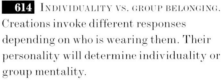
TRADITIONAL MANUFACTURING VS. EXPERIMENTATION. I like to find out why people did what they did traditionally and then experiment with it. You must remember that what we find traditional at the moment was once experimentation in the past. I think it is a good idea to have key pieces that represent the essence of the collection.

616 EVOLUTION. If you read, research, and experiment as much as possible it will be difficult not to improve every six months. My designs always have a sense of curiosity to them even though the materials, themes, and techniques are constantly changing.

617 IS FASHION ART? I do not consider myself a fine artist. However, I do create objects of beauty and deal with concepts that some people consider art. I prefer to call it fashion and research.

618 ADVICE. If you can't create what you want and making it seems impossible, consider then that maybe it does not exist yet and you have to invent it.

619 GOOD HABITS. Don't be afraid of failure, learn how to confront your weaknesses and have a financially secure business plan (this is much easier said than done).

620 ACKNOWLEDGEMENT. Inspiring others to live in a more sustainable way is the best praise I have gotten for my work.

leaf dress

falling flower top with falling flower skirt

621 INSPIRATION. I think about a mood I'm in at that time. I keep it close to how I feel or what I think about. Usually the start of a new collection is a reaction to the previous one. It can be a development from it or a step in another direction.

622 WORKPLACE. My workplace I got offered by the World Fashion Centre in Amsterdam. It is a beautiful, light space with two walls that are all windows and great sunlight in the morning. I arranged it in such a way to make it function for all of our needs. It's an atelier, office, showroom, and sometimes a café. I made it a personal space because I spend most of my time here, so I've got all my books, magazines, and some artwork here. And a very good coffee maker. Very important!

623 DEVELOPING A COLLECTION. A theme or concept very often translates to an embellishment like the hearts in my collection for F/W 09/10 where my love for creating fashion translated into different hearts and the current uncertainty of the financial market into the use of calico and drawings to still create a luxury, high-fashion look.

624 COLORS. Color is instinctive. I love to mix colors in a surprising, yet fitting way. They match very differently on all fabrics so I need to see a color on the actual fabric to choose it.

625 YOUR RIGHT ARM? My good friend Ehud Joseph, who I studied with at Central Saint Martins College. He studied menswear and has very different views so he's a good mirror for me.

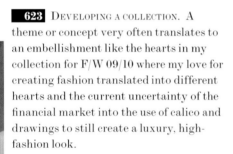

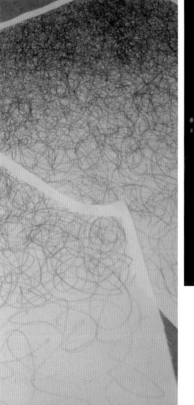

626 INDIVIDUALITY VS. GROUP BELONGING. I think individuality. For me the clothes I create are very personal, so I hope they'll look it when worn.

627 COMMUNICATION STRATEGY. Personality, quality, and luxury fashion. I think my communication is personal too. A label is also the person or people behind it.

628 STYLE. My style always balances between sophistication and edgy. It has a duality between a very constructed, tailored look and a softer, natural glamour.

629 SALES. Good fit, quality make and fabric, and exceptional design.

© Jan Bovenberg

© Jan Bovenberg

630
IS FASHION ART? I make garments to wear, not for a museum. I do think a whole show can be art because it expresses the epiphany of the idea of the collection.

© Haitze Spaanenburg

063 Mattijs van Bergen
www.mattijsvanbergen.com

During this time of global uncertainty, Mattijs makes a strong and decisive statement for both his inspiration and dedication to the art of creating garments and designing beautiful things. Like a blank canvas, Mattijs let the toile inspire him into creating pieces with clarity of shape and form, while being drawn towards more elaborate statement pieces. The heart-shaped details are an expression of Mattijs' love affair with fashion. This is his third ready-to-wear collection since his MA graduation from Central Saint Martins College in London in 2007. Mattijs followed his BA at ArtEZ, Institute of the Arts Arnhem. In 2006 Mattijs won the Modern Femininity award at the Lancôme Color Design Awards and participated in the Frans Molenaar Award. The following year, his graduation collection was nominated for the prestigious Harrods Award.

064 MJ Diehl, Roman Milisic/House of Diehl
www.houseofdiehl.com

The creative partnership of MJ Diehl and Roman Milisic, known as House of Diehl (HoD), is committed to producing statement-making fashion design and multimedia experiences. Their revolutionary work transcends the boundaries between fashion, art, music, and performance. House of Diehl has exhibited and performed their renowned, live, instant fashion shows for thousands of people around the world: with Sonic Youth and Rem Koolhaas at the Greenspace Festival in Spain; David LaChapelle and Gwen Stefani on her *Rich Girl* video; alongside Elton John, Liza Minelli, and Versace at the Lifeball, among others. They've been nominated for numerous design awards, winning the Triumph International Fashion Award 2004-2005. House of Diehl is also the inventor of Style Battling™, which has once again brought the fashion world to its feet.

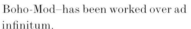

© Mimi Cabell

631 INSPIRATION. There's nothing more dangerous than playing it safe. Everything's been done—overdone. There's probably a stadium-sized hole in the ozone from another designer creating another little black dress. Get over it. HoD champions innovation over imitation, so we focus on process—an area ripe for innovation. Instant Couture™ and Style Battling™ are just two examples of our completely innovative design process, which has transformed the way people think about, produce, and experience fashion.

632 TRADITIONAL MANUFACTURING VS. EXPERIMENTATION. Decide if you want to be an innovator, or an assimilator. Now more than ever, there's nothing to be gained for a young designer assimilating to what's out there. Everything's been done. In fact, I see fashion entering its own "oil crisis." With 30 looks in 40 fashion shows in 12 fashion weeks twice a year that's nearly 30,000 looks being produced annually. Every combination of every standard theme—Grecian-Punk-Tudor-Preppie-

Boho-Mod—has been worked over ad infinitum.

633 INDIVIDUALITY VS. GROUP BELONGING. We consider them interlinked. House of Diehl uses fashion as a vehicle for a larger social agenda: individual identity, cross-cultural communication, and community. We strive to engage and edify the individual, while amplifying the voice of the greater community of which he/she is a part—local action that fuels a global reaction. Our continued mission is to create fashion that not only expresses a community, but generates one. We encourage you to be an individual, in a group of individuals.

634 BRAND VALUES. The personal resurrection of the makeover. The transcendence of fame. The fantasy of fashion. The integrity of art. The empowerment of authorship. The thrill of the spectacle. The satisfaction of the need to be heard, to be seen, to be loved—all around the world. We all want it all: HoD delivers it.

635
COMMUNICATION. Communication is everything. You not only need to be in complete control of your message, but you must be able to communicate it in a language that speaks to your audience. If your clothes could talk, would they mumble? Or are they the stand-up-and-take-notice shout-out to the world?

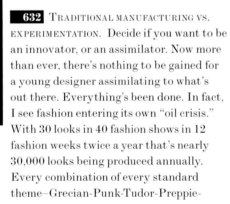

© John Gettings

© John Gettings

636 ADVICE. In a dream world, you've got six months to transform a beautiful bolt of silk into another little black dress. In the real world, your deadlines, resources, and budgets are tighter than Shrek in a Speedo. Be resourceful. Be relevant. Be willing and able to do anything, at any time, to further your work. And, most importantly, care…care about the environment, care about your client, care about starving kids somewhere, but make your work a "contribution" to society, and society will make a contribution to you.

637 WORKPLACE. Our workplace is a former strip club in downtown New York, now a full floor loft in which we work and live with our daughter. We live next door to Mariah Carey. It is part home, part showroom, part studio. There is a pink Jacuzzi installed by Wyclef Jean, the previous tenant, a Mae West lips couch, and a giant banana painted on the wall. The mannequins are display mannequins donated by Henri Bendel, but they simply give form to the real design work that takes place in our heads.

638 STREET FASHION VS. FASHION DESIGNER. Relevant fashion comes from the street trends. A good designer—one that actually instigates trends—is part soothsayer and part social analyst. He or she is acutely aware of what's going on in society and culture—not just today, but 20, 30, 40, 100 years in the past. That's because all fashion is an updated past look, reinterpreted for the modern world—fashion design is collagist art. In order for a collection to be embraced by the public—to speak for the public—it must be able to predict the future feelings of the public.

639 GOOD HABITS. Do your research. Ask to get paid upfront, or on delivery. Saves a lot of headache down the line.

640 MATERIALS. One of our primary fashion techniques is to break down and recreate clothing found at thrift stores or garage sales, to reuse their wonderful details and beautiful fabrics to make new, one-of-a-kind couture pieces—with no eco footprint. (It's also cheaper than buying the flat fabrics and unique notions!)

© John C. Liau

© John Gettings

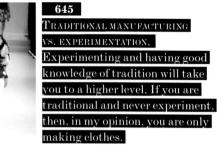

645
TRADITIONAL MANUFACTURING VS. EXPERIMENTATION. Experimenting and having good knowledge of tradition will take you to a higher level. If you are traditional and never experiment, then, in my opinion, you are only making clothes.

641 INSPIRATION. My collections always revolve around the "red line."

642 MATERIALS. I choose fabrics depending on their ability to convey the feelings I want to express. I buy them in France, Italy, England, China, and Japan. I never say "never" because mixes of materials and fabrics change with the times.

643 BRAND VALUES. Monique Collignon promises creativity, quality, and exclusivity.

644 COMMUNICATION. Our label is young, glamorous, feminine, high level, and a little bold.

646 EVOLUTION. You're only as good as your last collection.

647 STYLE. Every so often I stay with the most feminine, wearable, and detailed pieces, and I change the materials.

648 ADVICE. Be yourself.

649 GOOD HABITS. Be centered, persevere, perfect your patterns, have an overall vision, and communicate well.

650 SALES. Sales = wearability + price.

065

Monique Collignon
www.moniquecollignon.com

One of the Netherlands' most renowned designers, Monique Collignon is well known for her designs, her choice of materials, the processing of these materials, and the styles. This special formula always results in extraordinary and much talked-about collections. Her creations always "naturally" follow the contours of the body. Her client base boasts many successful and famous women. The haute couture items are designed and produced on the body. Every item is supplied with a carte d'authenticité, which guarantees the item's uniqueness. Next to her haute couture collection she also produces a ready-to-wear line: MC by Monique Collignon. Monique also produces specially designed creations and a great deal of bridal wear.

© Andrés Pérez Moreno

066

Mony Rivas/Chocolate
www.chocolateargentina.com.ar

The label was started in Buenos Aires in 1982, at the height of the Falklands war, with the aim of bringing hope, sweetness, and joy to the city. At the time, labels tended to have a name and surname, and Chocolate was a novelty, from its name all the way to how it displayed its products, its colors, décor, and advertising campaigns with international models, which made it into a legendary label of the nineties–so much so that Argentinean women would use Chocolate shopping bags as purses. The recipe for this candy-like establishment to keep up with the times belongs to two sisters: Mony Rivas and Susana Fandiño, whose secret is to create a silhouette with contrasting elements, in a balanced strategy combining the latest fashion with classic pieces. Their collections alternate between avant-garde designs, like anoraks, in technical fabrics and timeless pieces, such as knee-length tube skirts and romantic blouses.

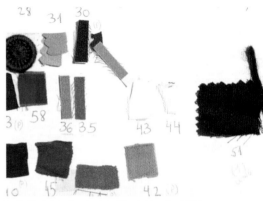

651 INSPIRATION. When I start to design a collection, to arrange it and give it form, there are so many things that go through my head. Themes, feelings, periods, and styles are mixed. What comes out of this mixture is a design that is later embodied in the clothes.

652 DEVELOPING A COLLECTION. The ideas and general concepts behind arranging a collection are materialized first in the search for a model silhouette. Then comes the exhausting task of experimenting with fabrics, textures, and colors. Those are the tools a designer has to use in order to turn a vision into a reality.

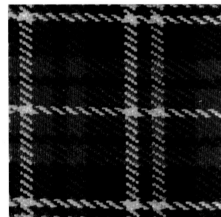

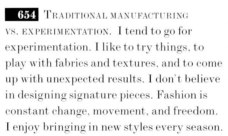

653 MATERIALS. I choose fabrics for their quality and texture, for the sensations they transmit. When I design a garment, I look for a suitable fabric in Argentina or anywhere else in the world. I like to vary, and I believe that all fabrics are good enough in themselves. The fact of using or ruling out a cloth depends on the particular styles I'm working with and the current trends.

654 TRADITIONAL MANUFACTURING VS. EXPERIMENTATION. I tend to go for experimentation. I like to try things, to play with fabrics and textures, and to come up with unexpected results. I don't believe in designing signature pieces. Fashion is constant change, movement, and freedom. I enjoy bringing in new styles every season.

655 INDIVIDUALITY VS. GROUP BELONGING. Chocolate clothes don't try to make people feel different, or to be members of a tribe, either. Our garments are designed for people to find their own style; for them to be more and more themelves. We want for them to feel comfortable in their bodies and for their personalities to be enhanced.

656 COMMUNICATION. I don't know whether you can talk of a "message" in a strict sense. Fashion transmits sensations. Chocolate is purity, simplicity, and versatility. It is both timeless and in flux. This is conveyed in both the choice of fabric and color ranges, and in graphics, displays, and packaging. The label's style is present in all things that go into making it up.

657 STYLE. I think that the style of a label is always the same. What changes is the trend. In our particular case, we try to innovate and present a different collection each year.

658 SALES. The important thing is to have an excellent product, in both looks and quality. Good materials and finishes are basic requirements. Excellent value for money is what will end up giving good results when the collection goes to market.

659 GOOD HABITS. Every designer has their way of working and their way of dealing with and adapting to national and international trends. It's vital that you be perseverant and always keep up your passion for what you do. This sacred flame is the engine that keeps everything running. It's essential to experience every season as if it were the first.

660

IS FASHION ART? Unquestionably, fashion is art. Dressing is a form of expression. It describes cultures, thoughts, and states of mind. Just like other disciplines in the art world, fashion works with colors, textures, volumes, and shapes. It's true that it's unavoidably linked to the market; but all of the arts are nowadays. It would be naïve to think of an art form that is remote from the reality of the market.

661 INSPIRATION. I first think of the way I am going to work the leather. Then I start looking around and I write my ideas on a big, white board to see them together. I select the way I am going to follow and I make up a story about the woman I dress. I imagine her wearing this new collection and where she goes, where she eats, what she buys, and her needs.

662 MATERIALS. I always buy the leather at the same tannery. I have been working with this material for twenty-five years and I understand the entire process. I go to the tannery myself and start working on them to make it exclusive, from the colors to the details.

663 COLORS. Brazil is a tropical country so color is very important here. I search for color everywhere–in a xbird, on a tree. I love strong colors like red, pink, and blue, but I also like leather colors too: browns, caramel, and nudes.

664 YOUR RIGHT ARM? Everyone is important in their own way for helping me. With my label, the factory is as important as the style. We make hand pieces and some of them cost me a whole day of production.

665 STYLE. I am always looking for new techniques to use on the leather for the way that it can turn out and look best (softer and thinner) and I always keep what my client needs as seasonal, like a good pencil skirt for example.

© Marcio Madeira

© Marcio Madeira

© Marcio Madeira

DESIRE

666 EVOLUTION. We have to be open to recycle, travel, and research and know what's happening in the world.

667 IS FASHION ART? I think so. Because I don't follow fashion, I search a new way to work with the leather first and then I go to the fashion, but what I really love is to challenge myself to the different kinds of things that I can achieve with the leather. The style and taste of each person is very unique and individual. For me, fashion is individuality. You can play with fashion to be who you are—one day you can be a rock star and on another day a hippie. It's up to you!

668 GOOD HABITS. Teamwork and shared activities.

669 SALES. Focus always on your client. You should know what they want even before they notice. The best praise for my work is when someone understands it as art.

670
COMMUNICATION STRATEGY. Retail is extremely important. I stay very close to my client in order to know what she desires and I spend time at the stores to observe what is going on.

© Sérgio Caddah

2004　　　　　　　　　　　　Sérgio Caddah

067

Patricia Viera
www.patriciaviera.com

A true prophet of Brazilian fashion, Patricia de Magalhães Viera began her career in the fashion business in 1979 in London, as the assistant of stylist Sally Mee. She returned to Brazil in 1979 and worked in Cia. Arte dos Pés as a shoe designer alongside Mauro Taubman until 1995. Ready for a new adventure, Patricia created her eponymous brand in 1998. The year after, in constant pursuit of bettering her style and global presence, she entered the international market with the English consultant Robert Forrest. Since 2004 the brand has been a part of the Brazilian fashion weeks, starting with Fashion Rio and the São Paulo Fashion Week. Her style is inspired by myths of folklore at the heart of the Amazon and popular knowledge–Viera's woman is feminine and sexy, but discards the vulgarity.

068

Petar Petrov
www.petarpetrov.com

Bulgarian Petar Petrov is based in Vienna where he studied at the Fashion Department of the University of Applied Arts. He has had his own menswear label since June 2002, and since June 2004 Petrov has managed to remain an official regular during the Paris Men's fashion shows. In January 2007 he launched his first womenswear collection. Both lines develop closely to each other, working with the same inspirations with the aim to create an aesthetical image, distanced from any ideological concepts. It is about contrast, the mix between high and low culture, elegance and street life. The style is elegant without being well groomed and stylish, without trying too hard, and intrigued by cultural differences and cultural force–the purity and simple aesthetic of forms mixed with the activity and vitality of life itself.

© York Weissmann

671 INSPIRATION. When I design I think about the many different people who might wear it, who have their own style, and who like being casual but at the same time sophisticated. When I design even the simplest piece, I make sure it is always a special item, one that has the right composition of material design to fulfill the person wearing it. I like my pieces to be unique and therefore that is what I think of every time I design one.

672 DEVELOPING A COLLECTION. I work intuitively. I design many different items at very different moments. In the end, to put together a collection I put the pieces I am most satisfied with. These items evolve differently from one to another and once an item pleases me, it inspires me for the next one, and so on. In the end, I think this is how I would define the concept of a collection, a related evolution of items, correlating to each other.

673 MATERIALS. I choose fabrics because I like them. I also choose them for their quality and even their innovation. I buy fabrics from all over the world. I always like experimenting with fabrics. Regarding the types…never say never. I think that everything can be used in a collection—it only needs to be placed in the right context.

674 TRADITIONAL MANUFACTURING VS. EXPERIMENTATION. I work with a mixture of traditional tailoring and experimental techniques. I think that every item needs to be representative.

675 INDIVIDUALITY VS. GROUP BELONGING. Both. Every item is a product. Some are more special than others but at the end of the day the aim is that all pieces are wearable and that they are a part of the collection in some way. This is the most difficult part of the creative process.

676 COMMUNICATION. Of course it's important, but I'm not involved in it. I have people that work directly with me and that help me take care of it. Communication nowadays is very important because somehow it becomes the image of the brand. The more you are out there, the more people want you. Unfortunately this is how it works. Therefore, as a business person, communication is essential.

677 EVOLUTION. I'm never satisfied with the result and I really try to make it better next season.

678 STREET FASHION VS. FASHION DESIGNER. Somehow both. The designers try to form the spirit of the street but the street reflects on the designers too.

679 GOOD HABITS. A combination of creativity and flexibility.

680 SALES. I hope that people wear my clothes and this is of course reflected in the sales but it doesn't exactly have a bearing on the creativity, it functions more as feedback.

681 INSPIRATION. I always begin the collection with an idea or a theme, whether it's a destination that I've been to or a place I dream of going, or sometimes it's about a girl and where she is going to. Let's face it, fashion is about dreams and fantasy with a dose of reality.

682 WORKPLACE. My workplace is separated into areas. I have a section where I keep all of my vintage archives and supplier information. Each supplier has their own box full of color and swatch cards from previous and current seasons that we refer to constantly. In the main design studio, we have mood boards up around the desks so that we are constantly reminded of our themes and colors.

683 TRADITIONAL MANUFACTURING VS. EXPERIMENTATION. I love to experiment! Sometimes it can go totally wrong but sometimes it can be quite successful. But that is the beauty of what we do. If we don't push the boundaries and experiment,

we will always be looking at the same thing. And that would be so boring.

684 INDIVIDUALITY VS. GROUP BELONGING. I believe that my customer is a leader more than a follower. She likes taking risks and she's confident enough to be the only one in the room wearing my designs. In fact, she almost prefers it that way. Of course when she meets another person who also has my bag, they are instantly connected and become friends. I love it when that happens.

685 COMMUNICATION. Marketing and communication is so crucial to making my brand stand apart from the rest of the crowd. I oversee everything that is communicated out to the public, from photo shoots to press releases. I have an in-house graphic designer that I collaborate with to realize my vision. I also work with an amazing fashion photographer, Micaela Rossato, for all of my ad campaigns.

686
COLORS. I always look for yummy colors and colors that evoke a mood or sensation. Sometimes a color that reminds you of food or a drink is a good thing! Mandarin orange, for example, is a very successful color for me, as is cognac!

687 EVOLUTION. As they say, you're only as good as your last collection. So at the end of every season, the cycle begins all over again. Sometimes I feel like the mouse in the pinwheel, but I'm still enjoying the run.

688 STREET FASHION VS. FASHION DESIGNER. It's the chicken-and-egg situation. Sometimes it can come from a designer and sometimes it can come from the streets. I believe that more and more often designers are watching what people wear on the streets.

689 ADVICE. Always follow your instincts but realize that, at the end of the day, it's a business. So indulge in your creativity but not at the expense of losing everything. Discipline, punctuality, curiosity, compassion, and humility. Oh, and a good accountant!

690 SALES. Designers don't live in an ivory tower. We must be true to ourselves but also listen and be open to ideas. If it makes sense, then do it. But if it feels wrong, follow your instinct and say no. Be aware of what is happening in the rest of the industry–keep your eyes and ears open. There is always a way to do it your way.

069 Rafe Totengco/Rafe New York
www.rafe.com

In 1989 Rafe Totengco left behind a successful clothing business he had started up in Manila for the chance to make his dream of being a part of New York fashion circles come true. He moved to the Big Apple and enrolled in the Fashion Institute of Technology.

In 1994 he brought out his first accessories collection–belts and watchstraps–for a Soho boutique. They soon sold out. When the store asked him if he also did bags, he quickly said he did, even though he had not even made one. His collection went on sale a year later. With the help of family and friends, Rafe had been able to expand his sales to 60 stores around the world by 1994. Since then he has become one of the most highly acclaimed of New York's new generation designers.

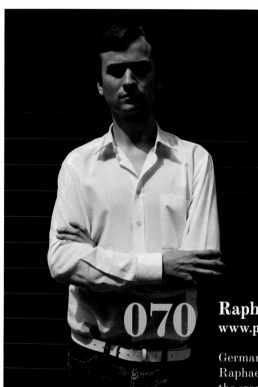

© Jan Lehner

070

Raphael Hauber/Postweiler Hauber
www.postweilerhauber.com

German designer Raphael Hauber is the creative mind behind Postweiler Hauber. Degrees in tailoring technologies at Niederrhein University and fashion design at Pforzheim gave Raphael the strong background to create his own label in 2003. He has taken part in shows at the Dune salons in Tokyo, Project Galerie, B&B, Ideal in Berlin, and Rendez-Vous in Paris. The press has been exceptionally receptive, featuring his work in publications such as *i-D*, *NEO2*, *Squint Homme*, and *Sleek*, among others. His latest collection is a collaboration between him and the artist Heinz Peter Kens. Images from the latter's archive were printed on the fabrics that make up this season's collection. Although commonly thought to be decorative, this collection focuses on the weight of the ornaments.

© Jan Lehner

© Jan Lehner

691 INSPIRATION. The theme is important, it has to be something that catches my attention at that point in time. There is always a conceptual part in the collection and a part that comes more through sensations and intuition.

692 WORKPLACE. My workplace is a bit chaotic with lots of patterns, our old lookbooks, and new inspirations on the wall—it changes from time to time. Our models have a special attitude and look (but not too special) in their appearance: angelic and pure.

693 MATERIALS. For me, the fabric has to be simple or casual and comfortable to wear, or it has to be a really special or technical treatment. Good quality is important. I like the combination of different fabrics, it is also part of my designs. As a young or independent designer, you have to lower your sights and look for alternatives as well, because you cannot buy such big amounts of textiles from suppliers—but this process can also be an advantage to your work.

694 TRADITIONAL MANUFACTURING VS. EXPERIMENTATION. Both are good. I am more traditional in the patterns: I prefer clear lines that you like to wear without complicated costumes. My experimental field is more in the use of fabrics, colors, and prints.

695 COLORS. The colors depend on the concept or come through my intuition. Color is important— certainly that is why so many designers also love black: black flattens and levels, it is neutral but has a strong image as well. Then the concentration is more on fabric, pattern, and the person wearing the clothes.

© Buck Ellison

© Buck Ellison

696 INDIVIDUALITY VS. GROUP BELONGING. I would not exclude either of them. There is this book called *Exactitudes*. In it are just pictures of different individuals of all those minority scenes and social groups like punks, skins, goths, etc. that all look the same because they use the same social codes and dress codes. If you asked them, they would say that they like to look individual but actually they all look like many others of that scene. I think for a person, it is important to belong to a certain group and this group characterizes itself through a special styling. Nobody will be a complete outsider of our community.

697 IS FASHION ART? That is open to dispute. The clothes are clothes to wear and maybe therefore not art in the common sense, but my approach and background can be compared to that of an artist. I have been repeatedly invited to join interspersing projects, e.g. the Museum of Contemporary Art, Karlsruhe, to show the work of Postweiler Hauber. The F/W 09/10 collection is a collaboration with the artist Heinz Peter Knes. In the last years, borders became fluid in this section. But there is still a strict line between fashion design and the art market.

698 STREET FASHION VS. FASHION DESIGNER. Fifty years ago, the big fashion trends came from the couture houses. Nowadays they also come from the street, stars, designers, and fashion magazines and blogs that filter all of them–it's an interplay. Some brands and designers are so influential that their vision of fashion sets the trends and affects what the masses are wearing.

699 ADVICE. Try it out as long as you are in school.

700 SALES. It's difficult to say in advance what is selling well and what is not. The bestsellers are mostly the more simple items but sometimes they are my most experimental pieces as well. I always try to include some of these simple and cheaper items . Regarding sales, those pieces are the entrance for a brand.

701 INSPIRATION. For me it often starts with some fabrics and colors, and then I work out from that.

702 REFERENCES. Everything. It can be music, art, kids...anything actually.

703 MATERIALS. I normally go on an inspirational trip to a new place before each season in order to keep up my "uniqueness"–I love using traditional, handcrafted fabrics and techniques from all over the world.

704 COLORS. I build up my color charts from moods and feelings that I want to express.

705 TRADITIONAL MANUFACTURING VS. EXPERIMENTATION. I have some items that I've had for more than one season; for example, my reversible bolero has survived four seasons in many different fabrics.

706
ADVICE. You are not really a success until you have been copied.

707 YOUR RIGHT ARM? All my employees, but I sit with my sourcing and production manager, Bente, and my construction girl, Tamiko, everyday and we discuss everything in the collection.

708 INDIVIDUALITY VS. GROUP BELONGING. I personally design out from the idea that I don't want to look like the others, which is why I use all unique fabrics and techniques. But of course, some of my customers probably buy my designs to signal some kind belonging.

709 BRAND VALUES. Individuality, new-thinking, quality.

710 IS FASHION ART? I make art, especially because I draw my own prints and paint my own backgrounds for campaigns and I try to have new and unique fabrics from all over the world each season.

071 Rikkemai Nielsen/Stories
www.rikkemai.com

Together with other Nordic countries, Denmark has been under the spotlight in the world of design for a long time, and that includes fashion design. An example of Danish talent is Rikkemai, based in Copenhagen. In 2008 she received the *Alt for Damerne* magazine Guldknappen (Golden Button) award for Best Danish Designer of the Year. Her clothes combine urban looks with boho, chic, vintage, and loads of style. Before starting each collection, Rikkemai travels to a different place in the world where she finds inspiration and collects unique fabrics, one of the features of the label. One example of how she makes use of them is the fabulous scarves from her highly successful F/W 09 collection, "Stories by Rikkemai."

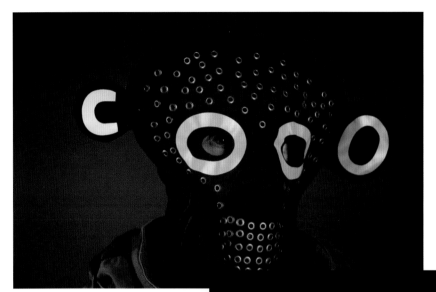

072

Rozalb de Mura
www.rozalbdemura.ro

Since 2006, the Romanian avant-garde fashion label Rozalb de Mura has been rediscovering fresh moments from the past, then setting them in utterly contemporary contexts–unflinchingly mixing real and imaginary characters and coolly playing with time and space. The memorable encounter between the eccentric character and designer Olah Gyarfas happened in 2006. Ever since, the contemporary style of the Transylvanian designer, impervious to short-lived trends and marked by austere cuts and exuberant details, found an ideal platform in the nonconformist aura of Rozalb de Mura label. The label draws its ideas from diverse references such as the music of the hip Swedish music duo The Knife, walks on a frozen volcanic lake, sci-fi movies, and Cretan cryptic notes.

711　INSPIRATION. When I start a new collection, I try to discover a "place" I've never been to. It can be disconcerting at the beginning; nevertheless, this feeling of being immersed in a new world fuels the imagination. Although my collections are generally built around a theme, I sometimes allow myself to be guided by intuition and sudden gusts of inspiration.

712　WORKPLACE. The quiet Transylvanian town of Miercurea Ciuc is far from the temptations of a big city. The pace of life is blissfully serene and out-of-time. My studio has chocolate brown walls and wooden benches, a lot of old frames, paintings, white porcelain, a fur–and manically ordered objects on my huge working table.

713　MATERIALS. It's the theme of the collection that dictates the choice of fabrics, from a very artificial and electro-glamour feel, with metallic or fluorescent colors in "A cracked smile and a silent shout" (2007) to an all black look in cashmere, tweed, and polyamide in "Thing" (2008). Plain, thin cotton is revisited. I often dip it in a coat of paint to give it the airiness of a dry leaf and the porosity and volume of paper.

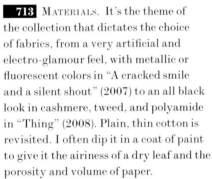

714　YOUR RIGHT ARM? It's much easier when one doesn't have to attend to all the not-so-creative aspects of a job. I'm lucky because I have a marketing team that I totally trust. I have great freedom but still need to take into consideration their opinion and respect some rules we established.

715

TRADITIONAL MANUFACTURING VS. EXPERIMENTATION. The past, with its fabulous costumes, artisans, and techniques is always a great source of inspiration. You churn it through your own personal philter and you get that unique, contemporary touch.

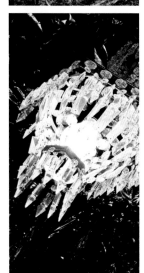

716 BRAND VALUES. Rozalb de Mura is the name of a fictional character we invented–mysterious, anachronical, generous, an enthusiastic traveller in space and time, passionate about art, music, nature, and science. The public is expecting the next dimension of the story that comes with each collection.

717 STYLE. I'm very eclectic in my choices. For example, I adore minimalism, and paradoxically enough, the flamboyant exuberance and foolishness of the eighties. The outcome might be described as a well-balanced mix of ideas, apparently classical cuts and unexpected details. I want my style to retain a contemporary look, with a vaguely perverse air here and there.

718 IS FASHION ART? In the twenty-first century, boundaries between fashion, art, and design became charmingly blurred. Rozalb de Mura is where fashion and art collide. In the latest project, we commissioned the British sound artist Mikhail Karikis to compose the music for our show at Ideal Berlin and OnIOff in London and he commissioned us to make clothes for his performances and a special drawing for his Morphica album.

719 SALES. My main concern is to tell a story and to communicate a vision, but I'm aware of the practical side as well: learn feedback, have a good mix of products, establish the right price. In Romania, there is not much support for developing a business in this field, therefore it's hard for a young label to build an international profile. Being in the right place (showroom, catwalk show) in the right moment helps a lot.

720 YOUR RIGHT ARM? People wearing the clothes and getting emotionally involved with Rozalb de Mura stories. Like a small community, we try to coagulate. Certainly, working with fabulous musicians and performers like Patrik Wolf, Brazilian Girls, Róisín Murphy, Loredana, Andi Vasluianu, or Anamaria Marinca is also a great reward of this work.

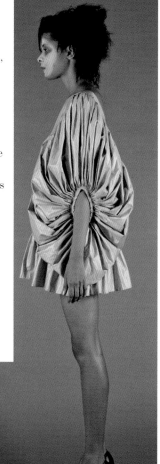

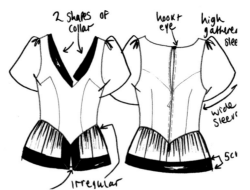

721 INSPIRATION. When referring back to what has influenced my collections it is easy to see how inspiration can be subconscious. Quite often I find that something seemingly insignificant can trigger a "starting point" for a collection. My concepts frequently relate to nature either through color or structures. I often feel inspired when in new, natural surroundings outside of a city.

722 DEVELOPING A COLLECTION. It is good to release what creative energy naturally brings to your concept, otherwise it can be stifling. It is important to research your themes and gain new knowledge on the concept in order to broaden your ideas and creative urge. I will often brainstorm many different ways to translate my ideas before selecting crucial elements to take forward into key detailing and silhouettes.

723 MATERIALS. Fabric is key to how a piece hangs and wears. It is one of the most important elements in my work and often a key starting point of inspiration.

Natural fibers are my preference; I rarely feature synthetic materials. I tend to stick to Italian and English fabrics for my outerwear and tailoring cloths as the woolens and cashmeres. In the summer, look to Spain for cottons and linens. I think it is important to source locally wherever you can.

724 TRADITIONAL MANUFACTURING VS. EXPERIMENTATION. It is always good to push boundaries; developing a product is never-ending and to experiment will only enhance your natural progression with any product. The craft of tailoring is always my reference point, so there is a lot of tradition in my cutting and structural design.

725 BRAND VALUES. When a customer purchases a piece of Evie Belle they are guaranteed something that is an investment in quality and style. The brand does not compromise on quality and customers appreciate that. We pay particular attention to detailing the design, to fabric, and to the make of each piece.

726 STYLE. We are a growing, affordable-luxury British label that promises longevity and is certainly not just a "flash in the pan." We have built a loyal customer base and with growing interest we can only expand to cover more areas of fashion and the luxury market.

727 EVOLUTION. It is good to evolve in many aspects of your life and it's healthy to regularly reassess each direction. I think it important early on to establish your handwriting and then improve certain aspects as you grow as a designer. Every designer is continually learning and therefore improving in some respect.

728 STREET FASHION VS. FASHION DESIGNER. Fashion and trends are two different entities. A street trend can be derived from varying subcultures in music and other art forms. Catwalk trends can also become diluted into high street trends, which is probably where the phrase "It's in fashion" is leaning towards currently. As any good designer knows, their work comes from inside not from following trends and it is only through analysis that certain trends across a designer's collection can be dissected.

729 SALES. Selling can be a struggle to many creative sorts. For a business to succeed and retain longevity as a brand, commercial awareness and customer targeting are key. You have to focus on creating new and interesting collections. However one cannot forget the pieces that will sell well to those satisfied, returning customers that love that particular product. Change for change's sake is not always necessary.

730
GOOD HABITS. Remain focused on your visions. Use inspiration combined with sensibility to create interesting, yet commercially viable collections. Always remain ahead of the game, be forward thinking, and lead, do not follow. Open up your mind to all sources of inspiration and use the things that you love to drive your passion forward. Take time to draw, paint, take photographs, take walks, travel, party, chat, laugh, and create.

073

Sairah Hicks/Evie Belle
www.eviebelle.com

When she was a child, designer Sairah Hicks was fascinated by *The House of Elliot*, a television show from the 20s about a young designer called Evie, a character who was behind Sairah's choice to enter the world of fashion. This is why, years later, when she set up her own label, the name Evie came quickly to Sairah's mind, accompanied with "Belle" to show that something beautiful was beginning. Her designs are mainly made in natural fibers like cotton, silk, linen, and wool, and are made in the UK as well as in other European countries. They are for a woman who understands elegance, sophistication, luxury, and the subtlety of details such as the buttons, fabric, and cut of a garment, and are stocked by exclusive boutiques in Europe.

© Jacqueline Di Milia

074

Samantha Pleet
www.samanthapleet.com

New York designer Samantha Pleet debuted her namesake collection for the F/W 06/07 season, intertwining elements of the dark, mysterious, and fantastical with a distinct sense of modernity. Her signature rompers, jackets, and chic day dresses are now best sellers at boutiques across the US and abroad, and she has developed a specialty in dressing indie bands such as Au Revoir Simone, Chairlift, The Pains of Being Pure at Heart, and Apache Beat. Since October 2008, she has designed an exclusive collection called "Rapscallion," which led to curating an Urban Outfitters pop-up store in Los Angeles in November 2008. She received a 2009 Ecco Domani sustainability design award for her work on the premiere collection of Bodkin. The 27-year-old Philadelphia native also paints, acts, makes films, and plans to start a band if she ever has the time.

731 INSPIRATION. I work very organically. My themes continue to develop all the way up until the last day before the show. It isn't until I have all the pieces that I really know what I was thinking.

732 WORKPLACE. I share a loft space in Williamsburg, Brooklyn with four friends: Tara of Covet, Susan of Dirty Librarian Chains, Eviana of Bodkin, and the photographer Jacqueline Di Milia. It's great sharing a space with these talented ladies because we all exchange ideas. In my office I surround myself with inspirational images, books, trinkets from my travels, and necessary design tools.

733 COLORS. I use color the same way I would typically use black in a collection. I want it to still feel "dark," even if it is a light color.

734 TRADITIONAL MANUFACTURING VS. EXPERIMENTATION. I love reinventing traditional clothing, like using details from nineteenth-century menswear, flannel shirts, and 80s rompers but combining them to make something new. I read history books and look through old periodicals and films for inspirational ideas from a long lost time or place. But I also think about what people want to be wearing now in their day-to-day lives, morning until evening, hot or cold. "Rapscallion," the line I design exclusive to Urban Outfitters, is a collection of very classic Samantha Pleet pieces. Each style is completely new; it really encompasses my ideals while being very wearable and sexy.

©Tom Hines

735
MATERIALS. The fabrics I favor are natural, vintage, recycled, and organic. I use them for their high quality and because they are sustainable. I also produce everything in New York City. It's important to me to support the local economy.

©AXVI

©Tom Hines

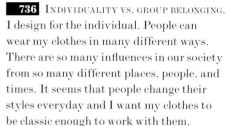

© Tim Zaragoza

736 INDIVIDUALITY VS. GROUP BELONGING. I design for the individual. People can wear my clothes in many different ways. There are so many influences in our society from so many different places, people, and times. It seems that people change their styles everyday and I want my clothes to be classic enough to work with them.

737 STYLE. My style is full of wonder and curiosity. I try to express this in each collection. Sometimes I will reinvent myself for a new season but the underlying influences are still there. My favorite films are watched over and over again from a different perspective, and then if I find something new and exciting I introduce it into the next season. I like addition more than subtraction.

© Tim Zaragoza

738 ADVICE. Don't try to make too many things. It is more important to pay attention to detail and do a few things perfectly. It's quality not quantity.

739 SALES. The key is to make silhouettes that may not be available everywhere, but that are what people are seeking. The hope is that when they see the piece, they buy it with a shriek of delight. Making the clothing saleable is the biggest challenge. You must focus on details in each of your designs–pockets, buttons, and fit–to make it as perfect as you can.

© Tom Hines

© Tom Hines

740 ACKNOWLEDGEMENT. I have been called a sorceress understudy, a butterfly farmer, and the queen of the romper.

741 INSPIRATION. Our themes always revolve around the cloth itself. In fact, Michael and I are in love with clothes of the past, the finishing, the details, etc. Our sensations are always the same: a desire of femininity and innocence, the desire to make the girl beautiful. We think about the girls we used to dress–new fabrics, new colors, new volumes, surprising but always recognizable.

742 DEVELOPING A COLLECTION. We have worked with the same model from the beginning. She has the innocence and the fragility of Audrey Hepburn, she has something very special in her look. She amazingly incarnates our universe.

743 WORKPLACE. We work in a huge place, a former printing house, located not far from the center of Brussels. It's very pleasant.

744 MATERIALS. Every season we go to Paris for the Première Vision trade fair. It's a fair where every fabric maker in the world shows his collection. Of course, we've worked with some fabric makers since the beginning of the label but it's always interesting to discover new ones.

745 TRADITIONAL MANUFACTURING VS. EXPERIMENTATION. Both are important, a mix of tradition and experimentation is very interesting. We love to use tradition and past knowledge for the finishing (regarding the making), but for the fabrics we really like to use new technical advancements.

© Emmanuel Laurent

746
INDIVIDUALITY VS. GROUP BELONGING. We don't want to do fashion effect as a kind of artifice. We really wanted to give our sensibility in a form of honesty. Our creations are made for girls who want to wear fantasy, something remarkable in the form of subtlety.

© Emmanuel Laurent

© Emmanuel Laurent

747 COMMUNICATION. Yes, of course. You can make the most beautiful collection in the world, but if nobody sees it then there was no need to do it. We have a press office in Paris and another one in Brussels working on our communication. We also have a commercial and press agent in New York.

748 IS FASHION ART? Not at all! We make clothes, original and different from mass-produced clothes.

749 GOOD HABITS. To be curious about everything.

750 ACKNOWLEDGEMENT. A recognizable universe, coherent and delicate. An innovative but wearable collection.

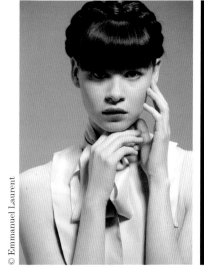

© Emmanuel Laurent

© Emmanuel Laurent

© Emmanuel Laurent

075

Sandrina Fasoli, Michael Marson/Sandrina Fasoli
www.sandrinafasoli.com

The creative duet formed by Sandrina Fasoli and Michael Marson is the spirit behind this new fashion name. Both graduated from the École Nationale Supérieure des Arts Visuels de la Cambre. Sandrina and Michael have their own vision of fashion, a very special approach based on unveiled femininity and melancholic innocence. This very vision of femininity brings national and international professional recognition and press coverage to the fashion duet (Grand Prix at the International Festival of Fashion Arts at Hyères, in 2003; Weekend Fashion Award, Modo Bruxellae Prize 2006; Mango Fashion Awards' finalist). Motivated by this professional recognition, they pursue their creative quest throughout the seasons and present several collections and projects, building up a signature style and a poetic and nostalgic mood.

076

Sarah Swash, Toshio Yamanaka/Swash
www.swash.co.uk

Sarah Swash and Toshio Yamanaka graduated from Central Saint Martins College of Art and Design in 2001 with a BA (Hons) in womenswear. They envisioned their eponymous label in 2004, and showcased their collection at Hyères where they won the Fashion Grand Prix and were awarded a further two prizes by the esteemed panel of judges. They have had two catwalk shows during London Fashion Week in 2004/2005—both sponsored by Topshop. They have worked on various projects that include designing a capsule collection for the French store 1,2,3, a film commissioned by Showstudio, and a collection of accessories with *Dazed & Confused* Japan and Garcia Marques. More recently they collaborated on a line of furnishings with the world famous shop Habitat entitled "Swash for Habitat," and in 2007 were one of the 10 selected designers in Mango Fashion Awards.

751 INSPIRATION. We begin by finding the theme or the objects that we will work with to create the collection. From there, we start the drawings and paintings. These are a very timely part of the process. The paintings are then put together into repeat prints, scarves, and placement prints for clothes.

752 DEVELOPING A COLLECTION. The concept of the collection does not have to translate into everything you design and trying to do this wouldn't be realistic. A collection will have an overall mood, or themes and details that will run through it. Often though particular garments will just be ideas you have been working on for a while or simply a shape that you like.

753 MATERIALS. We choose fabrics for different reasons. Usually we choose them after visiting fabric fairs or visiting factories directly. Often we select a fabric with the print in mind, something which will be responsive to color and go through the digital print process well. We like to use luxurious fabrics, particularly silks, which move well and feel beautiful to wear.

754 INDIVIDUALITY VS. GROUP BELONGING. Individuality.

755 TRADITIONAL MANUFACTURING VS. EXPERIMENTATION. A balance of tradition and experimentation is the most exciting, whether that be by using a traditional technique in a new way or re-working something very classic in a new yarn, color, or finish.

756 COMMUNICATION. It is definitely important to think about how you present your ideas in terms of a lookbook or photographs. It's also a very exciting part of the process and certainly something we work on personally.

757 EVOLUTION. Absolutely. That's part of the fun and excitement of fashion as you have the opportunity to present fresh ideas so often.

758 IS FASHION ART? No, fashion is not art. Fashion is made to be worn.

759 ADVICE. Making a collection isn't possible without a good address book of suppliers.

760 ACKNOWLEDGEMENT. Hearing from people who own it, love it, and wear it.

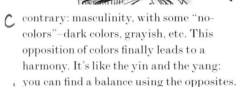

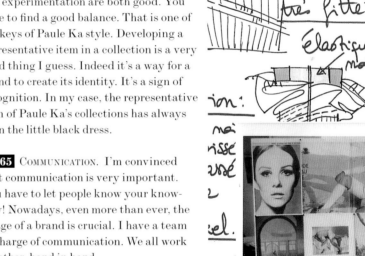

761 INSPIRATION. When I design a new collection I think of an elegant woman, sensual and relevant, who has a style. The emblematic women I think of are Audrey Hepburn, Jackie Kennedy, and Grace Kelly. Nowadays, Gisele Bündchen and Natalie Portman correspond well to the type of women I design for. Architecture is also a great source of inspiration for me. I'm an absolute fan of Oscar Niemeyer.

762 MATERIALS. I choose a fabric first, because of what it looks like, then because of its touch and its quality. I buy a lot of Italian fabrics. I can't say I will never use one specific fabric. Technical development is constant, and for instance some years ago I would have said I would never use a polyester, but nowadays they make some beautiful and really qualitative things with polyester!

763 COLORS. I'm looking for two things in color. First is femininity and happiness, with soft and bright colors. Second is the contrary: masculinity, with some "no-colors"—dark colors, grayish, etc. This opposition of colors finally leads to a harmony. It's like the yin and the yang: you can find a balance using the opposites.

764 TRADITIONAL MANUFACTURING VS. EXPERIMENTATION. I think that tradition and experimentation are both good. You have to find a good balance. That is one of the keys of Paule Ka style. Developing a representative item in a collection is a very good thing I guess. Indeed it's a way for a brand to create its identity. It's a sign of recognition. In my case, the representative item of Paule Ka's collections has always been the little black dress.

765 COMMUNICATION. I'm convinced that communication is very important. You have to let people know your know-how! Nowadays, even more than ever, the image of a brand is crucial. I have a team in charge of communication. We all work together, hand in hand.

766 EVOLUTION. Everyday I should say!

767 STYLE. The DNA of the brand remains the same collection after collection, so that you can find some recurrent pieces such as bi-material dresses, bi-color dresses, or high-waisted pieces. The things that change are techniques, fabrics, ideas.

768 STREET FASHION VS. FASHION DESIGNER. I think that there's a real exchange between designers and the street. A designer can propose something, and then the street can adopt and adapt it to its own style and desire. This reinterpretation of a piece can be a new source of inspiration for the designer. In fact, it's like a dialogue between people in the street and designers.

769 ACKNOWLEDGEMENT. The best praise for me is the loyalty of my customers who adhere to Paule Ka's style.

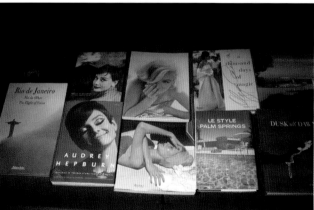

770 ADVICE. The best lesson I would like to share is that we can improve ourselves everyday. You have to remain humble. Pride is the worst enemy that a designer can have.

077

Serge Cajfinger/Paule Ka
www.pauleka.com

In 1987, Serge Cajfinger left Lille, France to start a new adventure. He established the Paule Ka label in the Marais area of Paris. A style code rapidly emerged: the use of black and white, which evolved throughout the seasons from monochromatic flashes to pastel tones. The skirt suit, the bow, the organza and the famous black dresses have remained the signature of Paule Ka for the past twenty years. Reflecting glamour from a Hollywood movie screen, but always set against an iconic Parisian backdrop, Paule Ka's style breaks through conventional ideas and plays with contrasts, volume, symmetry, humor, and seduction. The accessory collections express a timeless mood. The signature basket, created in 1995, has been reinvented each season.

© Sonia Sieff

078

Shenan Anddrommeda Fraguadas
www.shenan.us

An eccentric hundred-heir living in Greenpoint, Brooklyn, Shenan Anddrommeda Fraguadas cocked her eye and decided on a button fly. Only a few have been lucky enough to watch her work, and there was no contest. She was a woman possessed: music, outsider art, magic, beat writing, dreams, psychology, her two moms, friends, loves, crimes of passion, etc. Nothing was too much for her mirror, and she said she was always interested in working with new materials... across the room, a jack rabbit raised his ears. No need to scheme who she could dress, there was an assortment of success: Devendra Banhart, Bebel Gilberto, Turner Cody, Effi Briest, members of the Yeah Yeah Yeahs, the Liars, the Ex-Models. So the day came and went while Shenan paid a different kind of rent working at Mark Eisen, Uniqlo, Gap International, Steven Alan, and Calvin Klein.

772 INSPIRATION. When I begin a collection I allow myself to be a sponge and absorb as many sources as possible, tapping into both my own subconscious and the collective unconscious. I combine music, images from art and film, writing, experiences I have that have moved me, then collage it all both visually and psychologically.

773 DEVELOPING A COLLECTION. I translate the concept of each collection using symbolic imagery drawn from larger ideas. For example, in spring 2007 my concept was "Chairman Mao in the English Countryside" and I combined elements of peasant and worker clothing with quaint elements of the dress of a young girl living in the English countryside to show how these two concepts are at odds, but when combined visually they become interesting.

774 MATERIALS. I look for unique, modern fabrics. In the picture shown, the rayon fabric is heat-crinkled and acid washed to make it look beaten and worn. The rayon makes the piece drape easily. I would never use shiny spandex…it always looks trashy.

775 TRADITIONAL MANUFACTURING VS. EXPERIMENTATION. Tradition is an important resource to be mined: the ability to move forward is enhanced by studying tradition without allowing yourself to be trapped in it. The dress shown is a traditional smock dress, which is a representative item for me. It is totally sheer, incorporating elements of sexuality to a traditionally conservative piece.

771
REFERENCES. When I design I think of my friends that are artists and musicians, the person down the street who serves coffee, my mother, criminals, humanitarians…an amalgamation of the intelligent, the outsider, the leader: this becomes my idea of *she* and *he*.

776 BRAND VALUES. Since I do it to express myself I want others to feel free and unencumbered when they wear my clothes and to feel like they're creating their own world, as I create my own world when I make a collection. This is in combination with fine quality and workmanship.

777 COMMUNICATION STRATEGY. To appreciate the magical or surreal in the everyday, which allows both escape to another reality and the confidence to exist in your current one. My strategy is to infiltrate people's subconscious: your subconscious.

778 IS FASHION ART? Yes, I make art. I believe life is art.

779 STREET FASHION VS. FASHION DESIGNER. Fashion comes from the street, from daydreams, from history, from tribal symbols, from the world around us.

780 GOOD HABITS. A good designer should always be observing, absorbing, translating culture. They should try to avoid ego or pomposity, which just eats itself.

781 INSPIRATION. I transform various sensations into clothing. I take great inspiration from eras past. Just looking at photos from past decades I find fascinating, they can spark real creativity.

782 REFERENCES. For me, it is not so much a question of thinking as it is of feeling. When I am designing, it is ultimately an attempt to turn my emotions into a garment that not only captures but also radiates those emotions.

783 WORKPLACE. I have recently refurbished an old apartment into my new studio. Budgetary constrains meant that I had to keep it as simple as possible. However I made sure that I handpicked every little detail and that I really felt positive in the resulting environment. Feeling good in your workspace can really have a positive effect on both your mood and your work. I like to be surrounded by beautiful things. I try and have fresh flowers around as much as possible. Flowers have always been an inspiration to me.

784 MATERIALS. I work entirely with natural fabrics and mostly with different types of silk: chiffon, satin, raw silk, and duchess silk. I love silk. It feels so nice against the body and is the ultimate luxury. I believe that the best dresses do not only look great but also feel great. I would never use synthetic. I buy mostly from agents and distributors.

785 COLORS. Pastel palettes and soft colors are always an inspiration.

786 TRADITIONAL MANUFACTURING VS. EXPERIMENTATION. I would like to say that I consciously prefer tradition, but being self-taught is synonymous with having experimented your way through just about everything. So I guess a somewhat imbalanced mixture of the two works best for me. I don't really have centerpieces in my collections. In my opinion each piece should be amazing in its own way, yet all the pieces together should combine to form the collection.

787 BRAND VALUES. My clothes are feminine and have a romantic feel. Every one of us is unique—if your creations are inspired from within they can only invoke uniqueness.

788 STYLE. Quality, uniqueness, elegance, and always femininity.

789 ACKNOWLEDGEMENT. When my customers feel gorgeous in my designs!

790 ADVICE. As a self-taught designer, I can attest that if you have the talent, are willing to work hard, and believe in your passion, you will be well on your way to accomplishing your dream.

079

Sia Dimitriadi
www.siadimitriadi.com

Convinced that fashion should be beautiful, elegant, and ladylike, Scottish born designer Sia Dimitriadi creates irresistible garments. Sia launched her eponymous label in 2006. A self-taught designer, she takes a romantic approach to fashion. She adorns luxurious fabrics with unexpected details such as couture accents, adding personality to every piece. Inspired by the elegance of a ballerina and the seductiveness of bygone Hollywood boudoir, Sia designs collections of very individual pieces that are both ultra modern and timeless. Her trademark style is made up of cascading tulle and soft chiffon ruffles, voluminous ostrich feather embellishments, and hand-sewn clusters of tulle flower buds—all give life to dreamy textures. Delicate fabrics in ultimate black and hints of powdery shades help create a sought-after dramatic effect.

080

Simone Nunes
www.simonenunes.com.br

Simone Nunes–a lady blessed with the gene of creation. Since 2002, Nunes has dedicated her creativity and talent to the contemporary woman who shares the values of the brand–quality, comfort technology, and sophistication with strength and sensuality. Simone has exhibited her work at Amni Hot Spot, a vanguard event open to young Brazilian and international designers created by Paulo Borges, affiliated with the São Paulo Fashion Week. Through the years, her inspiration has outreached in many directions, from the geometric patterns to tropical warmth, always adding originality to her creations. Since 2006 the young designer has participated in various showrooms in Milan, São Paulo, Tokyo, and Paris, with growing international recognition for her unique style.

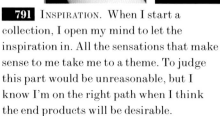

791 INSPIRATION. When I start a collection, I open my mind to let the inspiration in. All the sensations that make sense to me take me to a theme. To judge this part would be unreasonable, but I know I'm on the right path when I think the end products will be desirable.

792 DEVELOPING A COLLECTION. I translate the concept with the colors and shape, but mostly, I'm a figurative designer, so the embroideries are my best way to communicate my concepts.

793 MATERIALS. I choose the fabric by its structure; I like to work with fabric that behaves almost like paper, because of my square shapes. I usually buy them here in Brazil, but sometimes I import samples. There's no fabric I would never use for sure, because maybe in some future theme I'll need a different texture to communicate it, and it may be something that I dislike now.

794 TRADITIONAL MANUFACTURING VS. EXPERIMENTATION. My goal is to make some experimentation while maintaining some tradition; I try to maintain the image of the traditional with some new concept. Each collection has a representative item that can be recognized forever after.

795 INDIVIDUALITY VS. GROUP BELONGING. I think my creations invoke individuality due to the particular handmade image of the embroideries.

796 COMMUNICATION STRATEGY. I believe that a brand can be raised with all the technologies that we have today, but still with the human touch of handmade techniques.

797 EVOLUTION. I try to improve myself and my brand always.

798 STREET FASHION VS. FASHION DESIGNER. Nowadays, it happens both ways, depending on the brand target or strategy.

799 ACKNOWLEDGEMENT. The best one is "I must have this dress."

800
GOOD HABITS. We must insist, like working out at the gym, on making our inspiration obey time, so that you can improve and achieve the master creative collection–its deadlines and qualities.

801 INSPIRATION. I open my heart and my mind to the world, and find the things that connect with me. It's about transcending the obvious and seeing shapes that are interesting and complex. The planet is a rich visual source. I just try to open up and allow this sensory experience. Why not have faith in your own intuitive responses to the world?

802 WORKPLACE. My office is like a big case, where I keep photographs, pictures, and objects reminding me of places and images I love. I add to it constantly; it is a sort of memory bank.

803 DEVELOPING A COLLECTION. The main theme or inspiration is the feeling, the sensation you want to convey through the whole collection. This, like a crystal, has many faces–it's open to many interpretations and it can have many expressions in different products.

804 MATERIALS. Part of the fun of designing eyewear is playing around with textures and haptic effects: the combination of materials and colors formulate and inspire new languages. The secret is having an awareness of the energy they create with the curves and forms of your object.

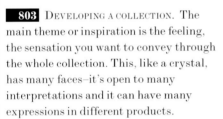

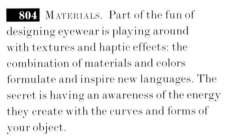

805 COLORS. The natural world provides something I am passionate about: contrast.

806 TRADITIONAL MANUFACTURING VS. EXPERIMENTATION. It's the only way to keep a brand alive. Curiosity is essential for our minds to seek out new ideas and possibilities. Let it lead you to new strategies, new materials, new technological solutions.

807 YOUR RIGHT ARM? I believe in collaborative work: the merging of minds, visions, ideologies, energies. I see design not like a profession but more like the attitude of thinking in relationships.

808 GOOD HABITS. Support culture. Next time you're going to the mall think about if you really need anything…then go to the museum instead!

809 MISSION. Making products that have a meaning, that are beautiful and stimulating for other people.

810 IS FASHION ART? I seek it in evrething I do. "Beauty is truth, truth is beauty," that is all. I see art as the vehicle by which beauty comes into our world.

adidas.com/originals

adidas®

081

Sonia Serlenga/adidas
www.adidas.com/originalseyewear

As an accomplished fashion and product designer, Sonia lists nature as her main source of inspiration and motivation. Nevertheless, daily city life, architecture, people, or a poem will equally influence her flair for design. Born and bred in Milan, Sonia graduated in product design from Politecnico and subsequently relocated to Linz, Austria to start her career in fashion and design. Here she initially worked for Lohberger before finally settling at Silhouette in October 2004. Her strength lies in research, a key part of her method. She claims to have always been a designer from childhood and what fascinates her in eyewear design is the possibility and the challenge to softly add the frames on a face, thus maintaining the harmony of one's features. A frame, according to Serlenga, says a great deal about the person who wears it.

082

Sophie Hulme
www.sophiehulme.com

A young UK designer, Sophie Hulme graduated in 2007 from Kingston University with Student of the Year and Best Collection awards. After much interest in her graduate collection she set up her own label two months later. Hailing from north London she now works from a studio in Islington. She uses masculine influences and hard detailing to give feminine pieces a new toughness. The result is a luxury look. The unique approach and style of the brand quickly gained interest. *The Telegraph* named her as one of UK's brightest talents. Sophie is currently working on several collaborative projects. Her first exclusive collection for Beams Japan has recently hit the stores along with a diffusion line for ASOS. She is also working with Jane Shephardson on the Whistles rebranding.

811 INSPIRATION. I always have a concept that we work toward. This is often very personal. I'm hugely influenced by my background and surroundings. I also like to go find old things with their own background and story to work from. I'm a massive collector–teacups, robots, glitter balls, bouncy balls, antique jewelry, vintage umbrellas, antique pencils, penguins…the list goes on!

812 REFERENCES. I don't tend to work with a specific customer in mind. I concentrate on each individual piece as an object and try to make them special in their own right.

813 MATERIALS. We go to Première Vision to source most of our fabrics. We have a real emphasis on quality so that's the most important thing to us when choosing them. I'd never rule out a type of fabric but we would never use machine sequinning–all of ours are hand-embroidered.

814 TRADITIONAL MANUFACTURING VS. EXPERIMENTATION. I think that a mix of tradition and experimentation is important–experimentation is far more interesting when it comes from a traditional, classic starting point. We always try to make everything a key piece–each should represent a strong idea. We don't make basics because, being a small brand, we think everything should have its own importance.

815
COLORS. The color is always an integral part of the design. Some pieces can take brighter colors while others need to be subtle. Great colors are really hard to find for sampling when you're a small brand, so we're always looking for something interesting.

816 YOUR RIGHT ARM? I work really closely with my assistant, Pete. We work on everything together. It's so nice to have a sounding board for your thoughts.

817 INDIVIDUALITY VS. GROUP BELONGING. I like the fact that my clothes are worn by all different types of people–men and women with all different styles. We don't like to prescribe how things should be worn. I hope that this means they invoke individuality. I like to see the different contexts in which people wear them.

818 BRAND VALUES. I hope it promises quality and something different. We always try to come up with new ways of doing things. We do make sure to stick to our aesthetic, which is very menswear influenced. I like to have this edge to womenswear. I hope it sets us apart.

819 SALES. Selling something unique makes for good sales, but it does need to be accessible and wearable or the customer will never buy it. This definitely informs my creativity. I like the challenge of creating something new and interesting that can still be worn and enjoyed by everyone.

820 ACKNOWLEDGEMENT. People wanting to wear it. There's nothing better than seeing someone walk down the street in one of your pieces.

821 INSPIRATION. It is really a very fluent process. We sketch ideas on a frequent basis. But before starting to design an actual collection we discuss many subjects, such as the political climate or socio-cultural movements; this is summoned to a certain sexuality, feel, or expression. When the overall theme is in place, we begin designing on a daily basis and discuss further.

822 DEVELOPING A COLLECTION. We develop nearly all samples in our atelier, from drawings over patterns, to fitting, to sale sample. When the collection is designed and constructed, we start to fit each piece on a model. Sometimes up to three different models with different body types are used. We do this to ensure a good fit even though the body may vary in proportions.

823 MATERIALS. We always try to get the various materials where the production is of high quality. We get a lot of wool from Austria and Italy, leather from Japan, silk from China, and cashmere from Mongolia. We always use high-quality materials. We design with a notion of comfort as well as a look and expression. The idea of "if you feel good, you will look good" is paramount.

824 TRADITIONAL MANUFACTURING VS. EXPERIMENTATION. You cannot have experimentation without tradition. Only when you have a tradition to break from you can develop your own. We love classic tailor-made suits, but we love even more to deconstruct and develop these further.

825 BRAND VALUES. We strive to make wonderful dresses and jackets in fantastic materials and a great fit–pieces with a perfect finish on the exterior as well as the interior.

826 COMMUNICATION. Communication is a vital instrument to getting people to see and feel your clothes. We work with press agents for media coverage. But even more important than press coverage, and that cannot be communicated in words, is the feel the wearer has when wearing a dress. This feel is communicated through body language.

827 IS FASHION ART? We address, in our own subtle manner, issues that preoccupy us. We don't feel we make art. Fashion has its own discourses.

828 GOOD HABITS. Feed your curiosity endlessly.

829 ACKNOWLEDGEMENT. To see somebody in one of our dresses dance the night away is fantastic! It is really refreshing to see people style our pieces in a personal way.

830
EVOLUTION. Personal development should be a constant. This is on a personal and a professional level. The social climate is an ever-changing sphere; one has to address this as often as possible.

083

Spon Diogo
www.spondiogo.com

Mia Lisa Spon and Rui Andersen Rodrigues Diogo live and work in Copenhagen. They have worked together as a design team for more than four years. After designing male and female prêt-à-porter collections, jewelry, bags, and identity programs for various companies, there came the recent decision to start their own project. Mia is a trained tailor and has worked for Danish and Swedish fashion and apparel companies; Rui is a self-taught arts entrepreneur that started out with a gallery and boutique in Reykjavik and was previously an arts editor for the Danish fashion magazine *III*. The Spon Diogo woman is urban, social, and strong. The approach to design is architectonic, structural, graphic, and strongly founded on a love for luxurious materials and detailed tailoring work.

084

Steve J & Yoni P
www.stevejandyonip.com

Korean-born Steve Jung and Yoni Pai have carved a reputation as fashion's newest prodigies. The design duo has shown at off-schedule London Fashion Week for four seasons, receiving international recognition. After meeting in Korea 10 years ago, Steve and Yoni shared a dream to start their own label, which became a reality when they moved to London to continue studying fashion. Steve completed both the BA & MA menswear at Central Saint Martins and Yoni completed the MA womenswear at London College of Fashion. Since winning the Best Menswear Award at CSM BA graduation show in 2006 and Samsung Fashion Design Fund in 2007/2008, Steve J & Yoni P have gone from strength to strength, being featured on the front covers of many international publications and also creating a distribution line for Topshop, all in a short space of time since launching.

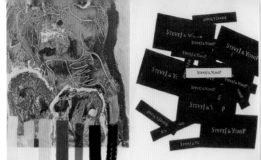

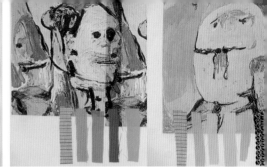

831 INSPIRATION. We spend lots of time researching to find inspiration and themes whenever we prepare a new collection. For the S/S 09 collection, we got the inspiration from architecture. So we have interpreted sculptural elements, such as metals and structured blocks, into a contemporary and modern look.

832 REFERENCES. Our design comes from our imagination and research. We combine our imagination with the new ideas from research and mold them into the garment. But we try to translate our concept into each item in an indirect way. To obtain these effects on the catwalk, we have combined elements of metallic mesh and textured fabrics, together with softer, colorful fabrics to get a more vibrant look. By making use of manipulation techniques, such as pleating and draping, we have attempted to introduce architectural factors into our garment, in an innovative and exciting new way.

833 COLORS. Fine arts! We were fascinated by Asger Jorn's beautiful paintings when we found them at Tate Modern last summer. The way of his color combination and childlike brush touch gave us a color inspiration. So we used orange, pink, and blue to form the base palette for the collection, with silver and gold as accent colors.

834 TRADITIONAL MANUFACTURING VS. EXPERIMENTATION. Our aesthetic would be "experimentation!" Trying new things and draping fabric onto a dummy is the best moment in the design process. We feel thrilled to find new and unexpected creations. We also think it would be a good idea for you to have some symbolic items every season that best represent your theme.

835 COMMUNICATION. Yes, communication is very important so that you don't mess up orders and every single aspect of the process. We think it makes the work process faster and more efficient in every business, even with creative artists. And we are in charge of it in our business as we control and direct our assistant, the workers and factory people, other material companies, etc.

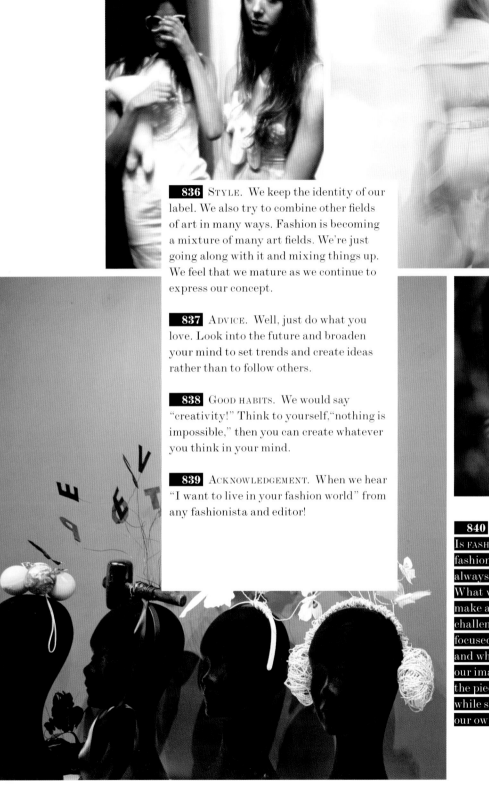

836 STYLE. We keep the identity of our label. We also try to combine other fields of art in many ways. Fashion is becoming a mixture of many art fields. We're just going along with it and mixing things up. We feel that we mature as we continue to express our concept.

837 ADVICE. Well, just do what you love. Look into the future and broaden your mind to set trends and create ideas rather than to follow others.

838 GOOD HABITS. We would say "creativity!" Think to yourself,"nothing is impossible," then you can create whatever you think in your mind.

839 ACKNOWLEDGEMENT. When we hear "I want to live in your fashion world" from any fashionista and editor!

840
Is FASHION ART? I can't separate fashion from art. They are always affecting each other. What we are doing is trying to make art wearable. The most challenging part is keeping focused on what is wearable and what is art—controlling our imagination—and making the pieces acceptable to society while still keeping it a part of our own fantasy.

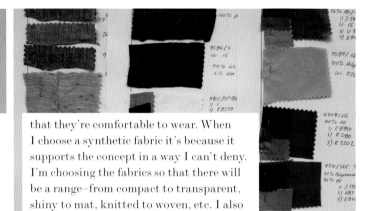

limbs of the p

841 INSPIRATION. I always have a theme when I start creating a new collection. I think it's important to build up a concept or universe and make it your own private space. The space will be the essence in which you create. In this way I'm convinced that you'll increase your creativity and develop innovative design.

842 DEVELOPING A COLLECTION. When I have worked out a concept I start collecting materials in connection with the subject. It can be visual materials from books, magazines, the Internet, pictures taken with my camera, or from written materials like newspapers, books, or the urban space, etc. It's a good idea to collect as much as possible and then sort it out later on and make the visual material more specific. Next step is to gather the visual material for a mood board in a sketchbook or on a blackboard. Last step, and the most important, is to translate this material into each item of the collection.

843 MATERIALS. First of all when I'm collecting fabrics for a new collection I look for natural fabrics like silk, cotton, wool, viscose, and so on. For me it's important

that they're comfortable to wear. When I choose a synthetic fabric it's because it supports the concept in a way I can't deny. I'm choosing the fabrics so that there will be a range–from compact to transparent, shiny to mat, knitted to woven, etc. I also try to incorporate ecological fabrics in each collection. There's one thing I wouldn't use though, and that's fur!

844 COLORS. I find my colors from my mood board. If I use colors besides black and white it's important that they're supporting the concept of the collection. Otherwise I prefer to keep it simple. Personally I think it's important that there's a reason why you're using the chosen colors.

845 INDIVIDUALITY VS. GROUP BELONGING. Mainly I think my creations invoke individuality. Most items from my collections have a twist, which makes the customer able to support their individuality, style, and image. Of course I have a customer target, but I want my clothes to be available to everybody who would like to wear them.

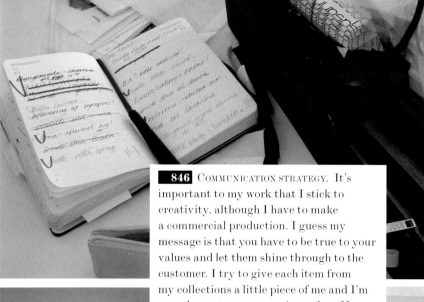

850
GOOD HABITS. Be open-minded, don't be afraid of sharing your knowledge, trust in your ideas and values, and have fun.

846 COMMUNICATION STRATEGY. It's important to my work that I stick to creativity, although I have to make a commercial production. I guess my message is that you have to be true to your values and let them shine through to the customer. I try to give each item from my collections a little piece of me and I'm sure the customer appreciates that. My communication strategy is quite simple. I want it to be open and vivid.

847 EVOLUTION. Every time I've finished a collection–and that regards every collection I've ever made, also from my time as a student–I want to improve myself next time. If you keep an open mind you'll learn all the time. I feel like I'm in constant development and that's really fantastic and something I appreciate.

848 IS FASHION ART? No, I wouldn't call my selling collections art, but I try to keep the balance between art and the commercial in a way that satisfies me. To me it's more important that I'm true to my concept. Besides that I always have a message for each collection. When you're a student, you're allowed to play as much as you like, but in the real world you also have additional need to sell your product.

849 STREET FASHION VS. FASHION DESIGNER. I believe that fashion has its outpouring in every individual that longs for "the new."

085

Susanne Guldager
www.susanneguldager.dk

A young Danish designer, Susanne graduated in 2007 with her MA in fashion from Designskolen Kolding, Denmark. The eponymous brand emerged on the fashion scene in February 2008. The design is developed from a conceptual and intuitive angle. Artistry, craftsmanship, and humorous elegance are the bedrock of all her collections, as well as avant-garde yet wearable clothing made of the finest quality. She is a curious interpreter of everyday life, and she has been investigating the crookedness that everything contains in her latest collection. For this reason her designs make use of asymmetry, making them unpredictable and interesting. A firm believer that the attempt to create an illusion of perfection is nothing more than destructive, she decided to shed perfect lines and shapes from her designs, thus challenging the illusion of the so-called perfect.

086

Takuya Miyama, Tomoko Kamijima/near.nippon
www.near-nippon.com

The company name evokes geographical references, but it is actually conceptual: near is used to bring an element closer to another end. Deeply rooted in tradition and holistic allusions, designers Takuya Miyama and Tomoko Kamijima believe that nature flows not from the center but from the linking of two circles. More specifically, they care to make universality and contemporaneousness coexist in their garments. Trends tend to wear thin and lose color. In the opinion of the Japanese duo, clothes take root in life and for this they never truly fade. This is reflected in their company image–the name and logo shows not belonging of each circle but balance at the junction. Near. nippon opened as a collaboration between the two designers in 2000, and right from the start Takuya took charge of the design concept and Tomoko cast his ideas into shape.

851 INSPIRATION. We always think about the harmony of directly-opposed ideas.

852 REFERENCES. Miyama thinks about season concept and designs. Kamijima makes patterns and silhouettes. Hattori (our assistant) makes details of clothes.

853 DEVELOPING A COLLECTION. We try to do it by the silhouettes and details of clothes.

854 MATERIALS. We choose them by the silhouette that wants to be made. We buy them from the trader who has treated materials of many companies. There aren't materials that I never choose.

855 TRADITIONAL MANUFACTURING VS. EXPERIMENTATION. We prefer experimentation. Yes, we think it's a good way to express directly-opposed ideas.

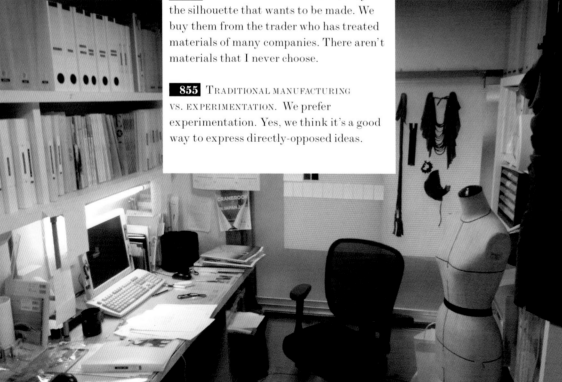

856 BRAND VALUES. We aim to create individuality. Our brand name *near* is coined to mean "to bring an element closer to another end."

857 IS FASHION ART? We think that the onlookers decide whether the collection is art or not.

858 ADVICE. Chat with people that have experience.

859 SALES. We don't know what makes for good sales.

860
COMMUNICATION STRATEGY. Our message is our collection. My communication strategy is to drink alcohol.

861 INSPIRATION. I decide the line the collection will follow depending on the feeling I have at the time. It all depends on the state of mind I'm in. I had a somewhat eighties street influence last year and I recently went back to much more glamorous and chic influences.

862 DEVELOPING A COLLECTION. I do all of the design work at home only, with music and television in the background–and with alcohol as an accessory. And it has to be alone and late at night. I need to be able to disconnect completely so as to be able to design, and that's only possible at home.

863 MATERIALS. All of my eyewear is made from cellulose acetate from the Italian company Mazzuchelli. Nevertheless, if I've been stocking standard colors for a few seasons, I rework them or I put them together to make new colors that will be exclusive to us and that will never be seen in other collections.

864 COLORS. The material and colors in a pair of eyeglasses are a means of conveying a message and a way of differentiating them from others. The work involved in the material is as important as what goes into the shapes. The same style in two different colors can convey diametrically opposed messages.

865 YOUR RIGHT ARM? I don't have any consultants in the design process. I design by myself. I don't listen to advice so as not to let it interfere with my creative processes. The same goes for my choice of colors. I normally have a solid idea of the result I want to achieve.

866 BRAND VALUES. The label is a synonym of quality because our eyewear is completely handmade in France, and different from a design point of view because the styles are clearly different from anything you can see on the market now.

867 COMMUNICATION. It all depends on the kind of publicity you mean. If you're talking about pages of advertising, then it's out of the question. I've never advertised my brand and never will. I don't like the idea of paying to show them in fashion magazines. I prefer to deserve it. On the other hand, if you mean media presence, well that's a different story. I have an absolutely incredible media presence when you think that I've had more than one almost daily appearance in the most important fashion magazines like *Vogue, W, L'Officiel, Marie-Claire, WWD,* etc. This regular presence is absolutely essential when you are an independent designer because it assures you, first, of buyers, and second, of customers.

868 ADVICE. Dare to be beautiful and to give off an allure. In terms of publicity, there is a double strategy: continued visibility in fashion magazines and a parallel market presence of the highest standard. You can't have one without the other.

869 IS FASHION ART? No, I wouldn't say I'm an artist, but I would say that some of my designs are clearly works of art that were designed with a purely artistic approach and without having to be toned down for commercial reasons. I easily imagine them in a museum rather than in a store.

© Peter Som 09

© Collaboration with Liquid Architecture and Thomas Lelu

870
EVOLUTION. If the collection is a success, or very successful, there is particular pressure on you in the lead up to designing the next collection because, naturally, you always have to do better, or at least as well. For the time being, I think about getting there and continuing to surprise (in a positive way) from one season to the next.

087

Thierry Lasry
www.thierrylasry.com

His sunglasses are setting the trend in the fashion world with their *futuristic vintage* concept, mixing classic looks with rock 'n' roll and electronic style. The collection reflects the image of its creator, Thierry Lasry, a young designer willing to share his inclination for modern design that combines charm and style with a slight touch of controversy. Thierry was raised in a world in which style and eyewear were one and the same. In this favorable background, he soon developed a liking for design that he put into practice with the release of his own collection in 2007. Thierry Lasry joins Paris Fashion Week every season, where he launches his new collections during the Premiere Classe Fashion Accessory Show in the Jardin des Tuileries in Paris. He also exhibits in several eyewear shows like Silmo in Paris, Mido in Milan, and Vision Expo in New York.

088 Tom Scott
www.tomscottnyc.com

Hailing from the Big Apple, Tom Scott is primarily a knitwear designer; his designs are characterized by architectural constructions that are simultaneously modern and understated, sophisticated and feminine. Previously, Scott was the men's and women's accessories designer for the Ralph Lauren collection. Under his own label, his work has been published in numerous publications, including *W*, *The New York Times Style Magazine*, *Harper's Bazaar*, *Papermag*, *Nylon*, and *Ryuko Tsushin*. In 2006, Scott's work was featured in the National Design Triennial at the Cooper-Hewitt National Design Museum. He is also the recipient of the 2007 Ecco Domani Fashion Foundation award. In 2008, Scott was nominated for The Australian Merino Woolmark Prize 2008, a prize that has been revived after 16 years by the non-profit organization, Australian Wool Innovation.

-fringe cape
-inverted sleeve dress

871 INSPIRATION. It's usually a question of mind over matter. I start with a distinct concept but sometimes a few ideas get tangled up together.

872 MANNEQUIN. I work with a size 6 girl on wheels.

873 COLORS. I look for shades of grey.

874 YOUR RIGHT ARM? Some of my pieces are just arms–and wish I had more of them!

875 BRAND VALUES. My name promises something that's unexpected.

-eyelet tee
-open side zip vest
-double shorts

-float stitch scarf

876
EVOLUTION. There's always room for improvement.

877 COMMUNICATION. I prefer to let my clothes speak for themselves.

878 PHILOSOPHY. Definitely, fashion comes from the street.

879 GOOD HABITS. I'm not the best example of good habits.

880 SALES. The best praise for my work is when someone can't wait to try it on.

TOM SCOTT

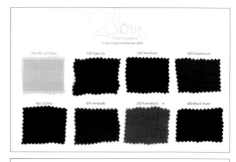

885 TRADITIONAL MANUFACTURING VS. EXPERIMENTATION. I'm always trying to evolve and push myself into experimenting. At the end, it always has the same signature without trying too hard.

881 REFERENCES. There is only that piece, the one I am designing at that moment, on my mind at any time.

882 MANNEQUIN. We drape and tuck on a dress form but always according to the original design idea.

883 COLORS. Life, history! My preference is for faded colors.

884 STYLE. Femininity with an edge.

TONYCOHEN

Prints Fall/ Winter 2009

PRINT A

PRINT B

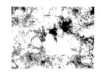

PRINT C

PRINT K

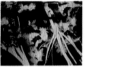

PRINT T1

PRINT T2

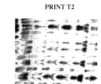

PRINT T3

886 COMMUNICATION STRATEGY. Integrity and individualism.

887 EVOLUTION. I need to push myself to perform, as does the competition!

888 IS FASHION ART? No, it is too fast for art, although it comes from the same place.

889 ADVICE. Stay as close to the original idea as possible!

890 SALES. It is a combination of factors, of which time is very important. It does not influence but it is taken into account.

089

Tony Cohen
www.tony-cohen.com

There are three things that made a career in fashion inevitable for Tony Cohen. First was being born in Amsterdam and growing up in the heart of the city, where the famous Waterlooplein Market is found. Second was his grandmother's passion for selling used clothes at this market (some of these vintage pieces are still in Tony's archive). And the third was the fact that his father worked in women's fashion for 40 years. After finishing his studies and spending a short time as a professional sportsman in the US, he moved to Italy where he began to make garment-dyed clothing. In 2004 he created the TONYCOHEN label, which was soon well received by international buyers of the likes of Harvey Nichols, Villa Moda, Lisa Kline, and Neiman Marcus.

090

Tracey Mitchell, Leigh Mitchell/Dahlia
www.dahliafashion.co.uk

The story begins with two devoted sisters: Tracey and Leigh Mitchell. Both coming from fashion backgrounds, they made the decision to stray from the high-street path and do their own thing: that's when Dahlia was born. Blossoming out of London's Portobello Market, the brand rapidly became an essential stop-off point for fashionistas and celebrities alike. Collections developed and grew with a distinctive style that was innovative, quirky, and girly. Proud of their roots, the unique clothing and statement accessories have a real British twist to them that play on traditional pieces, cleverly cut with fabulous prints and bespoke detailing. Styling mixes retro eras and trend-led inspirations to give Dahlia a real modern, eccentric feel that defines a look for a new generation of fashion devotees.

891 REFERENCES. I think about the silhouette I want to create first, then I work on the finer details. I imagine how the fabric will drape and how the shape will work on the body.

892 COLORS. I try to pick the color that represents the design best, but always thinking about whether it is flattering on skin tones.

893 INDIVIDUALITY VS. GROUP BELONGING. Individuality. Dahlia designs are inspirational and the attention to detail makes them unique.

894 BRAND VALUES. Unique, gorgeous, and lovingly-designed clothing that have lots of personality.

SHORTER VERSION

895
STYLE. We want to encourage women to have fun with fashion and feel special in their outfits.

896 EVOLUTION. I review the collection each season and learn from past mistakes.

897 STREET FASHION VS. FASHION DESIGNER. Being based in London, it definitely comes from the street.

898 ADVICE. Trust your instincts and don't believe everything you're told.

899 GOOD HABITS. Be very conscientious and make your ideas happen!

900 ACKNOWLEDGEMENT. Seeing Dahlia clothes being worn and hearing others compliment the wearer.

© Marc Castellet

901 INSPIRATION. When I begin a new collection, I think up an idea as a starting point and I work it through with my feelings to guide me.

902 DEVELOPING A COLLECTION. In order to transfer the idea of the collection to each piece I work mainly with patterns and fabrics.

903 MATERIALS. I choose the fabric that fits the collection I'm preparing. I mainly look at weight, body, texture, and quality. More than anything, I'm interested in shapes, so I generally work with non-color–black or white.

904 MANUFACTURING. A piece becomes a signature of the house unintentionally, although over time this symbol changes.

905 BRAND VALUES. The people who wear my clothes do so to feel like themselves. I think my label offers individuality and design.

906 EVOLUTION. In a way, I feel I have to outdo myself every six months, but, at the same time, I have quite a defined style and I don't like to throw away ideas I think are valid. Sometimes I keep on developing them to reach another point.

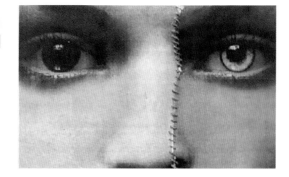

907 COMMUNICATION. Txell Miras has her own discourse and is willing to share it.

908 ADVICE. Beyond the purely academic side, it's essential to work hard and be passionate.

909 GOOD HABITS. Designers need to keep their eyes and minds wide open while upholding demanding standards and being true to their own personalities.

910 ACKNOWLEDGEMENT. The best applause is the satisfaction of a job well done and the good response of the people you trust the most.

© Marc Castellet

© Mirella Miras

© Hugo de la Rosa

091

Txell Miras
www.txellmiras.eu

The designer Txell Miras graduated from a fashion design course at the Escola Llotja in her native Barcelona in 2000. She completed a master's degree in fashion design at Domus Academy, Milan in 2001. Since 2003, Txell Miras has been designing the women's line for Neil Barrett.

Txell Miras started her own label in 2004. With it she has won a number of national and international prizes and shows every year at Barcelona's Pasarela Gaudí. Her interest in all forms of artistic expression has led her to experiment with disciplines outside of the world of fashion, like illustration, painting, photography, and even writing screenplays for short films. Duchamp, Bergman, Faulkner, Kafka, and Tarkovsky are the names she mentions when asked about the many different influences on the design of her collections.

092

Valentino
www.valentino.com

Whenever there is talk of fashion in the twentieth century, the name Valentino is always mentioned. From his first showing in the Palazzo Pitti in Florence in 1962 through to his last, presented at the Musée Rodin in Paris in early 2008, this Italian haute couture and prêt-à-porter designer was considered a living legend owing to his sense of beauty and elegance. His career was filled with numerous milestones, among which are his "Collezione Bianca" of 1968, his design for Jackie Kennedy's wedding dress when she married Aristotle Onassis, lending his name to the color "Valentino red," receiving the Neiman Marcus Prize only five years after his first showing, being named Cavaliere di Gran Croce in 1985 by the president of his country, and having been awarded France's Légion d'Honneur in 2006.

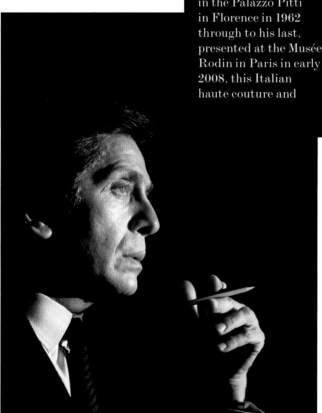

911 INSPIRATION. Follow your sensations. At the end, try to group all of them in a theme.

912 REFERENCES. Think to what you are designing: proportions, cuts, draping… not just the beauty of the drawing itself.

913 DEVELOPING A COLLECTION. It comes natural. You are the only one who has everything already in his head.

914 TRADITIONAL MANUFACTURING VS. EXPERIMENTATION. Evolution.

915 INDIVIDUALITY VS. GROUP BELONGING. Individuality and self-assurance.

916
BRAND VALUES. Show your real vision. Don't accept the ones of the photographer or the photo stylist.

917 EVOLUTION. A lot to retain, little to lose. What is seasonal is never good.

918 IS FASHION ART? Kind of art. The process is the same—me alone in front of a white paper, start to draw...this is art too.

919 ADVICE. Never read reviews on your collections.

920 GOOD HABITS. To be faithful to your own style and not follow the judgments of the press.

921 INSPIRATION. Naturally, we think of themes, feelings, emotions, and being able to materialize the combination of these things that exist inside of us with a great need to be expressed. We think of an ideal woman or man, and little by little we dress them with the aesthetic sense and philosophy we feel at the time.

922 WORKPLACE. When doing the women's collection, we work a lot straight over the body, and we have a model for this who we feel very comfortable with. We tend to work more with sketches for men's clothing. The space is Velazquez's birthplace, and our corner is the highest part of the house, where we enjoy the light and being surrounded by rooftops and domes of churches.

923 MATERIALS. We usually buy our fabrics from Première Vision (Paris). Others are specially made for us with our own participation, like the prints. Any fabric can seduce us, depending on the moment and the feelings we want to provoke. A classic noble fabric can fascinate us as much as an innovative one.

924 TRADITIONAL MANUFACTURING VS. EXPERIMENTATION. Both. But tradition always takes you to the greatest success. We developed a type of ruffle we call *caracola* (seashell) and have patented it.

925 BRAND VALUES. Our design strategy has always been at the cutting edge, but nurtured with the deepest cultural traditions, and this has given us a very particular style which makes us distinct. Our label promises authenticity.

927 COMMUNICATION. Fashion is communication in itself, which is why everything you contribute to it and that affects it directly is fantastic for the development of your label. We take charge of communication together with our team. What has always worked best is being coherent and true to ourselves; inexplicably, this is what is conveyed and reaches others.

928 STREET FASHION VS. FASHION DESIGNER. It used to come from designers' ideas; now it is very much imposed by urban looks, although it is always the designer who selects and transforms those looks.

929 ADVICE. Everything in life comes in due time; you shouldn't rush it. If you fight and are consistent, you achieve all of your goals in the end.

930 ACKNOWLEDGEMENT. The best thing is having our style recognized.

926
EVOLUTION. Until now, we've been lucky to still feel like children eager to learn; we feel the need to show what we do, and we want to improve and evolve, given that the career in design is infinite. The essence, the creative philosophy is kept, which is what the public has taken from you so strongly, and we imagine that what one is not able to convey is lost.

VICTORIO & LUCCHINO

093

Victorio & Lucchino
www.victorioylucchino.com

At the end of the 70s in Seville, local artist José Luis Medina del Corral and José Víctor Rodríguez, from Cordoba, began the Victorio & Lucchino project. Their idea was to make true their dream of a life where design would rule their work. From the start, there have been six elements defining the label's unmistakable representation: color; lace; fringing; the patented design of ruffles on sleeves, collars, and hems; wedding gowns (each unique and customized); and the fusion of the typical crafts of southern Spain with contemporary design.

094

Vidler & Nixon
www.vidlerandnixon.com

Stefan Vidler grew up on the shores of Perth, Australia, studying fashion tailoring in his hometown before setting his sights on London. With a talent for the visual arts, he carved out a career specializing in landscape painting and film. A chance meeting with Kerry marked his return to fashion with a range of intricate one-off pieces leading to their first collection for S/S 06. Kerry Nixon was born and raised in Glasgow, Scotland. She moved to London and graduated from the Guildhall School of Music and Drama in Violin and Electronic Music in 2001. Classical concertos and 24-speaker surround sound installations were her staple before turning her talents to fashion, for which she has been forever passionate. Combining her arts background with a love for everything vintage, Kerry seeks to create clothing that is both cutting-edge and elegant.

931 INSPIRATION. At Vidler & Nixon we work as a true design partnership. Before each collection, we both spend a month researching themes and inspiration. We then collaborate on the themes for each collection, creating mood boards and sketches. We both come from an art perspective and this influences everything we do. The initial concept stage is always a highly creative and exciting time.

932 REFERENCES. The Vidler & Nixon woman is elegant and sophisticated with a contemporary edge. We always keep the female form in mind and create clothing that is both cutting-edge and elegant. Our aim is to make women feel beautiful. We pride ourselves on having a fantastic, private clientele of women who come to us for special pieces and we enjoy being inspired by them.

933 WORKPLACE. Our workplace is a creative hub buzzing with people and ideas. We have a relaxed attitude in the studio as this promotes a good working environment and inspires quality design.

934 DEVELOPING A COLLECTION. Every piece in Vidler & Nixon has to feel like it is a little piece of luxury. From our original collaborations on intricate one-off pieces we realized the importance of quality and detail and have kept this our mantra throughout every collection.

935 MATERIALS. We use traditional Scottish fabrics for our coatings, beautiful luxury fabrics from Holland & Sherry, and hand-woven Harris Tweed. Driven by the desire to produce beautiful, high-quality garments, Vidler & Nixon have a true belief in their brand. We champion the use of luxury, traditional British fabrics by using them innovatively in womenswear. We have forged successful ties with the luxury Savile Row fabric house, Holland & Sherry, and develop and adapt their fabrics for womenswear.

936

BRAND VALUES. When you buy a Vidler & Nixon coat you are aware that you are taking home a new member of your wardrobe family–that it will stay with you forever and it will always be a statement piece without ever dating.

937 TRADITIONAL MANUFACTURING VS. EXPERIMENTATION. We try to strike a balance between tradition and experimentation. At Vidler & Nixon we like to keep one hand in the past and one in the future. We enjoy creating stand-out pieces in each collection such as the Marie Coat, a garment inspired by the flowing dresses of Marie Antoinette for A/W 2008. This item epitomized the brand, was worn by actresses on the red carpet, and gave Vidler & Nixon a distinct worldwide brand identity.

938 EVOLUTION. At Vidler & Nixon we try to keep a strong sense of brand identity by creating cutting-edge, elegant, and wearable garments. We are best known for our unorthodox tailoring and try to always retain the flair and sophistication that was our original trademark when we started the label. Our tailoring is very popular. We concentrate on the cut and line of our garments and always consider who we are making them for.

939 IS FASHION ART? Vidler & Nixon launched their first collection for women's wear for S/S 06. Their collaborations on exclusive and intricate one-off pieces established a trademark style of progressive structure and unorthodox tailoring that has continued through to their latest range. We started off by doing an entire collection of art pieces, structural pieces in felt, and intricate one-off garments and since then have kept tailoring our main focus. At Vidler & Nixon we like to convey the brand's identity by using many different art forms.

940 ADVICE. We realized very quickly that having good business and personal skills is key to the success of a young label. I think we have been successful in building Vidler & Nixon up in a short space of time because we work very hard to keep the quality of everything we show, produce, and market at its highest.

941 INSPIRATION. I build my collections around the materials. I make collages like children to keep track of all my ideas, and then I take them up again. The whole thing is always evolving.

942 DEVELOPING A COLLECTION. Transferring the concept of the collection to each of the pieces happens little by little like a skeleton. First comes the backbone with the main pieces, then the secondary parts go on. You have to be precise all the time; things should never get too jumbled up.

943 COMMUNICATION. Publicity is very important. It accounts for 40 percent of the development process of a collection. You shouldn't overlook this aspect. A very good collection can go completely unnoticed without effective publicity. It has to reach the consumer directly.

944 TRADITIONAL MANUFACTURING VS. EXPERIMENTATION. You need to know how to keep with tradition in making up a garment. The finish is very important. Likewise, you should turn to new technologies and new materials to enable your garments to evolve.

945 COLORS. I love color. It's the thing that conveys the most emotions. If you know how to play with it, you can be sure to reach the people who will love the piece. You need to know how to control it.

946 EVOLUTION. There is a unifying aspect that stays on from one connection to the next so they can be remembered, and so that my style can be recognized from season to season. You shouldn't throw buyers off by being too brutal and changing styles too often.

947 STREET FASHION VS. FASHION DESIGNER. Fashion is in the street. Each season designers reinterpret what the street brings to them in terms of new sensations. Even so, it is the designer who provides the first stimulus. One feeds off the other. It's a never-ending cycle.

948 ADVICE. Persevere. You can never take anything for granted in this business. Always be sure of yourself and never stray from your goals.

949 ACKNOWLEDGEMENT. The most encouraging response is what I get from the street, like the e-mails from people I don't know congratulating me on my work. Next is seeing myself and my work in the press. It does wonders for my ego, that's for sure. But the best response of all is people wearing my clothes.

950 GOOD HABITS. Patience. This is a business that tests your patience.

095

Vincent Schoepfer
www.vschoepfer.com

This young designer's studies at ESMOD in Lyon and then in Paris allowed him to develop his style and to refine his future professional choices. His intense need to create, imagine, and make progress led him to embark on a particularly original adventure. In 2001 he took advantage of the famous theatre festival of Avignon to set up a temporary boutique, "le garage des createurs," where he designed and made unique articles of clothing, with the idea of making his work and sensitivity known to a wider audience. Vincent's work is both colorful and retro. His casual-chic style, while based on a traditional, classical dress code, redefines the male image thanks to his bold and daring touch. Early in 2006, he presented his first men's collection at the young designer fair in Dinard, where he obtained the Mairie de Paris special award.

096

Virginia Spagnuolo/Divia Shoes
www.diviashoes.com

One day, lawyer Virginia Spagnuolo decided to study drama and her life changed forever. It made her see that her true vocation was in a more creative field: shoe design. She handcrafts them in Argentinean leather and in limited editions. Intricate as a honeycomb and with cutaways and heart-shaped stones or diamanté buckles, they are sold in the Palermo district of Buenos Aires and Asia. Virginia says of herself, "Shoes are everything to me; I've always been fanatical about them. Once I asked Santa Claus for bubblegum pink shoes instead of a Barbie doll. Every style has its story, like my souvenir peacock from a trip to India, or the fans I played with as a little girl. My work is playful. My designs come from my fantasies." This is why when she makes black shoes, they don't work.

951 REFERENCES. Everything I design carries a little part of my life. My shoes are inspired by childhood memories. They are the moments from it. That's why I say they have a soul. My main reference is my grandmother, Victoria, a fighter and an independent woman for her time. I still have her Singer sewing machine and treasure it as if it were a sculpture of her.

952 INSPIRATION. I find great inspiration in travel. For me, design is directly linked to my feelings. Everything I design has something to do with my fantasies and my need for expression.

953 COLORS. I like to play with the combination of color and texture. It's a distinctive feature of my shoes. I love to create figures, like butterflies and hearts. Each style has many details; I'm no minimalist and I never will be.

954 BRAND VALUES. Divia promises passion and love for a lifetime.

955 WORKPLACE. My work space is both chaos and organization. Chaos, because I believe the best ideas come from it; and organization, so as to be able to materialize my ideas and make them real.

956 IS FASHION ART? What I do is directly related to my expressiveness. I communicate my feelings, my joys, through my designs. I feel this to be my art.

957 ADVICE. You should always do what you're passionate about; believe in your projects; use perseverance and intuition; and do it with love, because that's the most important source of inspiration.

958 SALES. Sooner or later, everything you do with passion, love, and dedication is reflected in your sales and in the growth of your label. I feel I can prosper with authenticity and intuition.

959 INDIVIDUALITY VS. GROUP BELONGING. The women who choose my designs have a strong personality and are extremely sensitive. They love to be different.

960 ACKNOWLEDGEMENT. The greatest acknowledgement is when my clients feel the same happiness when they wear their Divia shoes as I do when I design them.

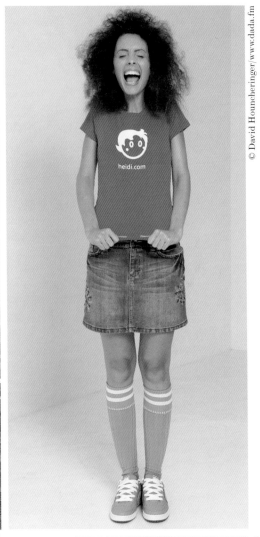

961 ADVICE. Take care about first opportunities. Try to work in person on that kind of business.

962 DEVELOPING A COLLECTION. It follows each product. We try to put a touch of it on all of the designs, but the most important part is placing the theme on our T-shirts.

963 COLORS. We choose four to five colors for each gender, so we try to find two original tendency colors from the fashion industries and two classic colors, such as black and white.

964 MATERIALS. The fabrics depend on the products, so we do not choose a product for a fabric but rather a fabric for a product.

© David Houncheringer/www.dada.fm

© David Houncheringer/www.dada.fm

965 EVOLUTION. From time to time we try to understand what people want instead of thinking of what you prefer–so that you understand the market better.

966 CHALLENGE. We do what we can, we try to give our best always…so you automatically improve yourself each day. The best praise for my work is when I like to wear my products.

967 WORKPLACE. Our home and headquarters is in Neuchâtel, Switzerland, near a wonderful lake, where Alpine roots meet urban creativity.

968 COMMUNICATION STRATEGY. Guerrilla marketing, interesting and funny marketing operations. Have a look at http://www.streetwear.ch/guerrilla/index.html.

969 SALES. They do not influence the concept of the collection, but yes, a little bit on the choice of the products.

970 BRAND VALUES. The value of Heidi.com is a trinity between pure alpine roots (Heidi), creativity (logo), and worldwide openness (.com). We are group-oriented.

© David Houncheringer/www.dada.fm

© David Houncheringer/www.dada.fm

097

Willy Fantin, Andreas Doering/Heidi.com
www.heidi.com

Heidi.com saw the light toward the end of 2003 thanks to Willy Fantin and Andreas Doering, two daring young men from Switzerland who decided to fuse together in a brand that combines Johanna Spyri's famous children's book character and twenty-first century aesthetics.

Heidi's values were recontextualized to fit perfectly in a contemporary urban environment. Their first outlet was the Web, but the products quickly attracted retail interest. Heidi.com grew steadily to embrace a collection composed of T-shirts, hoodies, jackets,

dresses, caps, belts, and lots of accessories. The values of the brand are a triangulation between pure alpine roots, creativity, and worldwide openness. As of today, over 120 shops successfully sell Heidi.com products throughout Europe.

© Drakopoulos

098

Yiorgos Eleftheriades
www.yiorgoseleftheriades.gr

Hailing from Greece, this designer has created 40 women's and 22 men's collections that have been presented in Athens, Paris, London, Milan, and Berlin. Based on his love for classical forms and in search for contemporary elegance, he aims to create a truly alternative urban style with interesting shapes, strong tailoring, and experimental combinations of fabrics and textures. He is fond of bringing together contrasting materials–the mat with the glittery, the high-tech with the retro, the masculine with the feminine, the luxurious with the utilitarian. Colorwise, each collection is based on a palette of neutral shades, followed by a strong scheme of intense colors. The result is often offbeat and striking. The main quality of his designing perception is a trans-seasonal timelessness and a glamorous but cool day-to-night approach.

971 REFERENCES. Mostly the shapes and the attitude of the collection.

972 MANNEQUIN. For the house model I use a girl named Genevieve. She is super stylish with a great sense of beauty. My workplace is a big space, full of light and good energy.

973 COLORS. I look for the feeling, the tension, and the balance.

974 TRADITIONAL MANUFACTURING VS. EXPERIMENTATION. Something in between.

975 STYLE. Every collection is defined mostly by the forms and the fabrics.

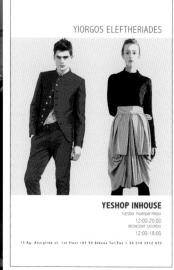

© Nikos Vardakastanis

YIORGOS ELEFTHERIADES

YESHOP INHOUSE
TUESDAY THURSDAY FRIDAY
12:00–20:00
WEDNESDAY SATURDAY
12:00–18:00

13 Ag. Anargiron st. 1st floor 105 54 Athens Tel/Fax + 30 210 3312 622

© Vassilis Karidis for *Look Magazine*

976 INDIVIDUALITY VS. GROUP BELONGING. Individuality, I hope…

977 COMMUNICATION. Communication is important for fashion in general. I am represented by Totem press office in Paris.

978 STREET FASHION VS. FASHION DESIGNER. The creativity in fashion comes always from a need which has to be filled. So, both!

979 ACKNOWLEDGEMENT. The difference, the diachronism, and the comfort.

980 ADVICE. You have to be patient with creativity.

© Vassilis Skopelitis

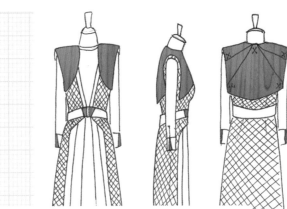

981 INSPIRATION. When I start a collection, I first think of my own feelings and experiences, which I put into order. Then I relate them to more general and abstract concepts. During this process I let some ideas go while others come to me that seem more suggestive. As I develop them, little by little, they give me the theme for the collection.

982 DEVELOPING A COLLECTION. For me to work on a concept, I do thorough research on different areas that interest me, like art, movies, psychology, and medicine, until the time when I'm just about to design, when I stop researching so as not to let myself be conditioned. After that, all the images and ideas that have occurred to me are embodied in the prints. I match colors bearing in mind the psychology behind the colors. I choose the right fabrics for the garments I'm

interested in and define the right shapes by carefully analyzing the patternmaking process, so that when everything's brought together, the resulting clothes are coherent with the concept.

983 COLORS. My collections revolve around sensations and feelings, which is why I choose colors depending on the psychological aspects and associations they suggest. I place a good deal of importance on the psychology of color, because of the information it provides, and in order to achieve an overall coherent collection.

984 YOUR RIGHT ARM? All of my friends with so many different backgrounds such as medicine, engineering, architecture, and photography, among others, are interested in my work. They get involved and give suggestions and help with a total lack of self-interest because they believe in this multi-disciplinary project.

985 BRAND VALUES. It's not that people feel different or defined as part of a group in my clothes; rather, it's the conceptualization of the entire design process, and the material, forms, and the iconographic nature of the prints that make each piece part of a story that has to be imagined by the person wearing it. They are a distinguishing feature and an accomplice to our emotions.

YYY GUTZ

© Nacho Gabrielli

© Abad Fotografía

986 COMMUNICATION. Communication is an essential part of fashion. Besides a press office that plays an essential role in communication and PR, I use other, more novel Internet-based channels; each channel reaches a different audience. I always supervise communication personally so that, whether through the press office or outside of it, it's always suitable for the label.

987 EVOLUTION. It isn't a matter of whether to change or continue. My work is a kind of development that more often than not begins in a different place and has unexpected goals. Despite the fact that there are always new ideas behind it, concepts and forms inevitably appear that coincide with other collections, although they do always end up developing in an irregular way.

988 Is FASHION ART? I don't think of my work exactly as art. However fashion, like art, is a form of expression, and I've chosen it as my means of expression.

989 GOOD HABITS. Perseverance, humility, and enthusiasm.

990 ACKNOWLEDGEMENT. The best praise is what your fellow professionals give you; the praise that comes from people who work for fashion, directly or indirectly, because they acknowledge and value the difficulty inherent in a project, which makes it doubly gratifying.

099

Yiyí Gutz
www.yiyigutz.es

Yiyí Gutz belongs to the latest wave of young Spanish designers who are transforming the local fashion scene with their innovative and risqué designs. Right from the start of their design process, Yiyí Gutz clothes are inspired by their designer's interests—art, science, her most intimate thoughts, and especially her feelings— and reflect her graphic design experience in their prints, small series of geometric shapes, and flat colors created exclusively for each collection, which give the clothes a strong symbolic content. Her collections have appeared at different runway shows in Spain for three years now, obtaining various prizes and mentions. She also collaborates in different disciplines of art and design.

100

Zazo & Brull
www.zazobrull.com

Xavier Zazo and Clara Brull use their collections to tell stories. They believe clothes have more than a functional role of covering and protecting the body; they feel it is a way of expressing the way people are and feel. Based on their own personal experiences, they have created an imaginary world where a new character is created each season. Their inspiration for this is in the tenderness found in the work of Joe Sorren, the mixture of innocence and perversion in Mark Ryden's illustrations, and the infinite imagination of the characters created by Tim Burton. Since their beginnings in 2000, Zazo & Brull have shown their collections at Barcelona and Madrid fashion weeks, and at international fairs such as Ideacomo (Como, Italy) and the International Fashion Fair held in Tokyo.

991 INSPIRATION. Behind each of our collections is a story that has made us think, imagine, and feel. We always try to convey the feelings we have experienced so that people can enjoy our clothes to the fullest.

992 DEVELOPING A COLLECTION. We use certain details from our inspiration, whether they are tangible or not, and we develop them until we find the desired shapes and/or textures so that we can successfully make our clothes.

993 COLORS. Black, beige, and red are constants in our collections. Each one in and of itself has a value (plus they complement each other). Black brings sobriety, red brings passion, and beige brings elegance.

994 TRADITIONAL MANUFACTURING VS. EXPERIMENTATION. Both tradition and experimentation are essential. The former provides the best ways of doing things, and the latter lets you achieve what you never thought could be done. The signature piece of each collection is the one that is impregnated with the essence of the concept. And it's from this that the rest of the line is broken down.

995 BRAND VALUES. Zazo & Brull promises to be the lead character of a new story each season.

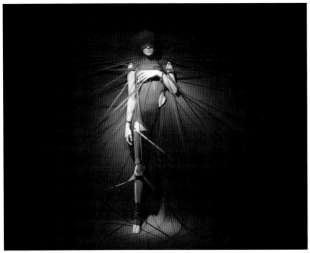

996

EVOLUTION. Your design has to evolve every six months, but always within the limits of your style. This growth is very personal, and not everybody might appreciate it, but as a designer, it must give you the confidence and security of knowing you are on the right path.

997 COMMUNICATION. This is essential. Our clothes bear the message of our label, which is the experience of the new, of being a part of a story. The red on our labels shows there is passion in our creations and that clothes aren't just clothes. It's value added that people who identify with our clothes notice. We are always behind our messages.

998 IS FASHION ART? We believe fashion is highly connected to art, and that all of its variants can express all kinds of concepts.

999 GOOD HABITS. A designer must soak up everything life has to offer because inspiration can come from any mundane experience that makes you reflect or feel.

1.000 ACKNOWLEDEMENT. When people use our clothes for their personal or professional projects.

N TAGEMOSE

JOE SORREN

MARK RYDEN

EUGENIO RECUENCO

WIN OLAF

MUSEU DEL JOGUET

RAY CAESAR

DOU

ACKHEART GANG

STEPHANE HALLEUX

ELIZABETH MCGRATH

RAI ESCALE